Bilingual
Guide
to Japan

JAPANESE POTTERY

SAWADA Mieko

JN048511

SHOGAKUKAN

Bilingual Guide to Japan
JAPANESE POTTERY

SAWADA Mieko

Book and Cover design ©Kindaichi Design

Published by
SHOGAKUKAN
2-3-1 Hitotsubashi Chiyoda-Ku,
Tokyo 101-8001 JAPAN
https://www.shogakukan.co.jp
https://japanesebooks.jp/en/

YAKIMONO BILINGUAL GUIDE by
SAWADA Mieko
©2020 SAWADA Mieko
SAITO Naomi / SHOGAKUKAN
Printed in Japan
ISBN 978-4-09-388795-3

やきものバイリンガルガイド

澤田美恵子　著

小学館

English Renderings of Pottery Terms

This English and Japanese bilingual book introduces the basic knowledge and representative types of Yakimono (Japanese pottery).

All Japanese terms are rendered in italicized Roman characters. The only diacritical to indicate long vowel sounds, and the hyphen (-), to separate two adjacent vowel sounds or polysyllables.

H: Height
D: Diameter
BD: Body Diameter
MD: Mouth Diameter

Since the conventions for rendering these terms into English differ depending on the facility, terms used elsewhere may not be consistent with those used in this book. Given that even Japanese names and pronunciations may differ depending on the sect or region, they cannot be generalized. Standard names are used in this book and are rendered so that they can be easily read by individuals who are not native speakers of Japanese.

本書の英文表記について
この本は、代表的なやきものについて紹介しています。日本語が母語ではない人のために、英語で訳してあります。
日本語はローマ字読みにし、アルファベットで表記しています。母音が続く場合や多音節語にはハイフン (−) を使用しています。

※これら外国語表記は、施設（公共施設、地方自治体等）ごとに異なるルールで表記されているため、本書と一致しない場合があります。地方によって日本語でも呼び方が異なることがあり、一般化はできません。本書では標準的な呼称を掲載し、外国語を母語とする読者ができるだけ平易に発音できる表記としました。

Table of Contents 目次

Introduction

What Is Japanese Pottery?

Pottery is the product of nature's blessings, such as fire, soil, water, and human hands. Different parts of the world have developed distinctive forms of pottery that reflect their peculiar history, culture, and climate. Despite the arc-shaped island of Japan is small in size, the climate, plants and animals in the south are vastly different from those in the north. As a result, the soil differs from region to region and this, combined with the local history, has led to the creation of unique wares.

Jomon pottery is said to have originated in Japan almost 12,000 years ago and is considered the oldest form of pottery in the world. Since its birth, pottery's long history unfolded alongside those of the people, who shaped clay for various uses, for example, as idols to pray god, as containers for food, or works of art for the heart's contentment.

Japanese pottery is closely related to the country's eating habits. For example, Japanese people tend to have a personal rice bowl, for

はじめに

●日本の陶芸とは

　やきものは、火と土と水という自然からの恵みと人の手によって生み出され、世界中にはそれぞれの歴史や文化、風土を色濃く映した特色あるやきものがあります。弓なりの形をした島国の日本は、小さな国でありながら、南と北では気候も、生息する植物や動物も異なります。そのために地域によって土も異なり、歴史の物語もあいまって、色とりどりの個性豊かなやきものが誕生しました。

　約1万2000年前の日本には、縄文土器が存在したという説があり、この縄文土器が世界最古のやきものと考えられています。それは時に神に祈るための人形、時に食べ物を入れる器、はたまた人の心を満たす芸術品など、さまざまに形を変えて、人とともに長い歴史を歩んできました。

their own exclusive use. Since the bowls are held in the hands and used every day, people choose them not only by color and pattern but also for their texture, size, and weight. The bowls must feel ideal for use, resulting in the pursuit of something specific to meet individual taste. Pottery wares related to food have, therefore, become even more diverse and versatile in order to enrich and add color to our lives.

Enjoying the World of Pottery

In the 21st century, with the development of artificial intelligence and 3D printing, what is the significance of making objects by hand? This book introduces handmade pottery to find the answer to this question. Each ware in the world is unique. By learning the history behind each piece, you will be able to fully understand and appreciate the object you hold in your hands.

The more you learn about pottery, the more enjoyable it becomes. The more you are exposed to pottery, the more it will

　また日本の器作りは、日本人の食生活と深い関係があります。たとえば、日本人は自分専用のご飯茶碗をもっています。茶碗は毎日手にもって使うので、色や文様の好みはもちろん、手触りや大きさ、重さといった身体に寄り添う好みも選択の重要な条件になるため、使い手にとって心地よいものづくりが追求されてきました。こうして食と関係する日本のやきものは生活を豊かに心地よく彩るためにも一層に多様で多彩なものとなったのです。

●やきものを巡る旅の楽しみ

　21世紀になり人工知能や3Dプリンターが発達したなかで、人の手でものをつくる意味とは何でしょうか。その解を探るためにも、この本では手づくりのやきものを紹介していきます。手づくりのやきものは世界でただ一つのものです。やきものの背景にあ

warm your heart. This book introduces the art of Japanese pottery and its production sites and was written in the hope that it will encourage you to experience the natural beauty and encounter the people of those areas. However, if you cannot travel for some reason, I hope you will at least enjoy this virtual walkthrough the world of pottery.

I hope this book will be your gateway to discover Japanese pottery and embark on your own exciting journey.

Sawada Mieko, Ph.D.
Professor of Arts and Science, Kyoto Institute of Technology
Critic of Arts and Crafts

る物語を知ることにより、あなたが手に取ったやきものは、実にたくさんのことをあなたに語りかけてくれるに違いありません。

　やきものは知識を得れば得るほどに、楽しさが倍増します。そして、心を込めてつくられたやきものに出会えれば、そのやきものは、あなたの心をきっと温かく包んでくれることでしょう。本書は、日本のやきもの魅力とその産地について紹介するものであり、日本のさまざまなやきものの産地を巡り、地域の自然や人、そしてやきものに出会ってほしいと願い執筆しました。しかしながら、あなたが今、何らかの事情で旅が許されないなら、せめて仮想のやきもの散歩をして楽しんで下さることを願っています。

　本書が日本のやきものと出会う入口となり、あなただけの心躍る旅が始まることを祈念しています。

澤田美恵子
京都工芸繊維大学工芸科学研究科教授、博士（言語文化学）、工芸評論家

Chapter 1

Basic Knowledge of Japanese Pottery

第一章

やきものの基礎知識

History of Japanese Pottery

Early Earthenware

It is no exaggeration to say that Japanese pottery has maintained the world's highest quality from the oldest known forms of pottery in the Jomon period (12,000 years ago) to contemporary ceramics.

Earthenware was originally made of clay mixed with pebbles and sand, decorated with patterns and fired at 600-900°C on flat or hollow ground. The richly decorated vessels are thought to have been used in rituals. Works with flame-like ornamentation (p. 12), whose design closely resembles burning flames, evoke a sense of fear, proving that the concept of art already existed in Japan as far back as 4,500 years ago. The richly decorated vessels are thought to have been used in rituals.

From the 3rd century onwards, almost all ornamentation disappeared in favor of the unglazed hazel-colored earthenware, known as "Haji pottery."

日本のやきものの歴史

●土器の誕生

　日本のやきものは、世界最古といわれる約1万2000年前の縄文式土器に始まり現代陶芸に到るまで、世界最高水準の質を保ち続けてきたといっても過言ではないだろう。

　まず最初に登場した土器は小石や砂などを混ぜた粘土を成形し、文様で装飾したのちに、平地やくぼ地で600〜900度で野焼きしたものだ。燃え上がる焔（ほのお）を思い起こさせ、恐れすら感じる造形の火焔型土器（p.12）は、4500年も前にこの国に芸術が存在したことを証明している。豊かな装飾の器は祭礼用と思われる。

　3世紀頃からは装飾がほとんどなくなり、土師器（はじき）と呼ばれる赤褐色の素焼土器へと変わっていく。

From Stoneware to Pottery and Porcelain

In the 5th century, a new technique of firing at 1,000-1,200°C was introduced from the Korean Peninsula, stoneware was made from iron-rich clay in kilns at around 1,200°C. Known as "Sue pottery" (p. 13), high-fired gray stoneware with a runny green ash glaze began to emerge. This is said to be the beginning of pottery.

By the second half of the 7th century, low-fired pottery, made with clay that has been refined to remove impurities, covered by green-glazed using artificial glazes (see *yuyaku*, p. 120) were produced. In the 8th century, earthenware with three-color glaze (p. 14) were made using not only green, but also yellow and brown glazes; high-fired pottery flourished. However, it would take nearly another thousand years for porcelain to be produced in Japan, as a high level of skill was required. The raw material for porcelain is porcelain stone or a combination of porcelain stone and clay, fired at 1,300-1,400°C. The early type of porcelain can be seen in 17th century Arita ware.

●炻器から陶器、そして磁器へ

　さらに5世紀に入ると朝鮮半島から1000〜1200度で焼成できる新しい技術が伝わり、鉄分を多く含む粘土を原料に、窯を用いて1200度ほどで炻器がつくられた。須恵器 (p.13) と呼ばれる自然釉で青灰色の硬く焼き締ったものが、その始まりとされる。

　7世紀後半になると、精製して不純物を取り除いた粘土が原料の低火度陶器に人工的な釉薬 (p.120) を使った、緑釉 (りょくゆう) 陶器が生まれた。8世紀には緑だけでなく黄色と褐色の釉薬が使われた三彩陶器 (p.14) も製作され、高火度陶器の全盛を迎えた。しかし高度な技術が必要な磁器の誕生までは、さらに約1000年の月日が必要であった。磁器の原料は陶石、あるいは陶石と粘土を合わせたもので、1300度前後の高温で焼成される。17世紀の有田焼に初期の作例が見られる。

Deep Bowl with Flame-like Ornamentation
3000-2000 BC / H 35.0cm /
Tokyo National Museum

か えんがた ど き
火焔型土器
前3000〜前2000年／
高35.0cm／東京国立博物館

Sue Pottery
8th century / H 34.3cm / Kyushu National Museum

須恵器　多嘴壺
8世紀／高34.3cm／
九州国立博物館

Source：ColBase(https://colbase.nich.go.jp)　13

Jar with Three-color Glaze
Important Cultural Property / 8th century /
H 13.7cm, BD 21.3cm / Kyushu National Museum

な ら さんさいつぼ
奈良三彩壺
重文／8世紀／
高13.7cm　胴径21.3cm／九州国立博物館

　Source: ColBase(https://colbase.nich.go.jp)

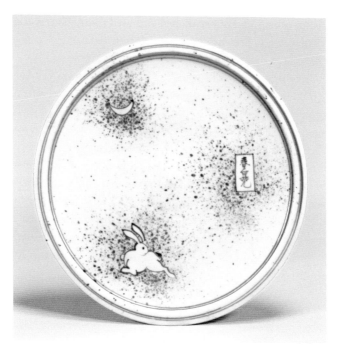

Dish with Underglaze Cobalt-blue Design of Hare and Moon
Arita ware / 17th century /
D 19.9cm / Tokyo National Museum

そめつけふきずみげっと ず さら
染付吹墨月兎図皿
有田／17世紀／
径19.9㎝／東京国立博物館

Source: ColBase (https://colbase.nich.go.jp) 15

Materials
Characteristics of the Soil

One way to determine the history of a specific area is to listen to the voice of its soil. Pottery shaped and fired using the clay from a particular region presents a unique coloring and somewhat reveals the history of that region.

For example, Shigaraki ware (p. 18) is made from the soil of Shigaraki, which is located south of Lake Biwa in Shiga Prefecture. Approximately four million years ago, the Shigaraki area was covered by the lake, therefore, the stratum is now rich with fossils of shellfish that once lived in the lake's water. Around the 13th century, people who became aware of this excellent soil began to make pottery. When Shigaraki soil is molded and fired using the ancient methods of pit kilns (p. 120) and Japanese multiple-climbing kilns (p. 120), the areas hit by the flame turn red and emit a unique vermilion color called "fire color (scarlet)." In the kiln, the ash falls on the surface of the vessel and melts, turning it green or yellow and giving it a unique flavor.

素材——陶土の個性

　その土地の粘土を形にして焼いたやきものは、その土地の歴史を物語り、その土地独特の色を醸し出す。

　たとえば信楽焼（しがらきやき）(p.18) は、滋賀県の琵琶湖の南にある信楽の土でつくられたやきものだ。約400万年前、湖の底だった信楽には、かつて淡水に生息した貝類の化石を含む地層が広がる。その地層に火山岩の風化物が流れ込み良質な陶土となった。13世紀頃には、柔軟性にすぐれた土質の良さに気づいた人たちが、やきものをつくるようになる。信楽の土を成形し、穴窯 (p.120) や登り窯 (p.120) という古来の手法で焼くと、炎が当たった部分は赤くなり、火（緋）色と呼ばれる独特の朱色となる。また窯の中では、器の表面に降り掛かった灰が、素地の成分と混ざりあ

This process, of firing wares at high temperatures without applying a glaze to coat the surface and changing the firing color depending on the firewood ash in the kiln, is known as "*yakishime*." These works typically depict natural sceneries on the clay using the natural color of the soil and the flames.

On the other hand, Bizen ware (p. 19) is dark brown and has a dull luster. While it is also made using the *yakishime* technique, even at first glance, its color looks different from Shigaraki ware. Bizen city, located in Okayama Prefecture, enjoys the mild climate of the Seto Inland Sea and is run through by the Yoshii River. Approximately 3 meters beneath the fields, lies a layer of high-quality soil known as "*hiyose*," which is composed of the rich soil washed away from the mountains more than a million years ago. It is a sticky soil containing iron and must be slowly fired at 1200°C for about two weeks. After this time, the clay becomes smooth, firm, and robust.

って、緑や黄色となり、特有の味わいを醸す。このように人工的に釉薬をかけずに、高温で焼き、窯の中で降り掛かる薪の灰や炎によって焼いた色が自然に変わるものを「焼締め」と呼ぶ。焼締めはまさに土と炎が生み出す自然の景色だ。

　一方、備前焼（p.19）は、焦げ茶色で鈍い光沢がある。同じ焼締めではあるが、信楽焼とは一見して土の色が違うことが分かる。岡山県にある備前市は、温暖な瀬戸内海の気候で、吉井川が流れる地だ。田畑の地下およそ3mには、100万年以上前に山々から流失した山土の一部が堆積した「干寄（ひよせ）」と呼ばれる良質な土の層がある。鉄分を含む粘り強い土で、1200度で約2週間ゆっくりと焼き締めなければならない。その時間のおかげで、やきものは滑らかで固く堅牢となる。

Large Jar with Natural Glaze Design of Higaki Pattern
Shigaraki ware / Late 14th century-Early 15th century / H 42.0cm /
Agency for Cultural Affairs, Government of Japan

Large Jar with Natural Ash Glaze Design of Incised Lines
Bizen ware / 15th-16th century /
Tokyo National Museum

<ruby>自<rt>し</rt></ruby><ruby>然<rt>ぜん</rt></ruby><ruby>釉<rt>ゆう</rt></ruby><ruby>刻<rt>こく</rt></ruby><ruby>文<rt>もん</rt></ruby><ruby>大<rt>たい</rt></ruby><ruby>壺<rt>こ</rt></ruby>
自然釉刻文大壺
備前／15〜16世紀／
東京国立博物館

Differences Between Earthenware and Porcelain

The feeling you get when you hold a bowl in your hands is a message from the earth that directly reaches your heart. The majority of the pottery we use in our daily life are earthenware (p. 22) and porcelain (p. 23), but even within the same white bowl different messages are conveyed.

Earthenware is thicker with small holes and, when you hold it, it feels a little lighter than it looks. Porcelain, on the other hand, is thin and its surface is smooth to the touch, leaving a cool sensation on the hand. Moreover, if you hold a piece of earthenware out to the sun, the light does not pass through it, unlike porcelain which allows light to penetrate and the pattern shows through. Earthenware is made of clay, while porcelain is made of porcelain stone, which contains a high ratio of silicic acid. The latter also can be used as the base material for glass and light differently penetrates through it.

When snapped, earthenware makes a dull sound, while porcelain makes a soft, metallic sound. When warm tea is poured, earthenware transmits warmth slowly and gently, while porcelain instantly conveys the temperature to the hand that holds it. Also,

陶器と磁器の違い

　手の中にすっぽりと茶碗を抱えたときの感触は、心に直接届く地球からのメッセージだ。現在私たちが生活のなかで用いるやきものの大半が陶器 (p.22) と磁器 (p.23) だが、同じ白い茶碗でも両者が発するメッセージは異なる。

　厚みがあって細かな孔 (あな) があるほうが陶器で、手に取ってみると見た目より少し軽く感じる。一方磁器は、薄くて表面が滑らかで、触るとつるりとしており、手にひんやりとした感覚が残る。また、太陽にかざしてみると、陶器は光を通さないが、磁器のほうはうっすらと光を通し、透かした文様も現れる。陶器の素地 (きじ) の原料は粘土層の土、磁器はガラスの素にもなる珪酸の比率が高い陶石を原料に使っているため、光の通し方も異なるのだ。

as earthenware has small holes on its surface, if something with a strong pigment, such as *matcha* (powdered green tea), is poured in it will gradually seep into the base material and the color will change over time, giving it a richer flavor. On the other hand, porcelain, like glassware, is impermeable to water.

The firing temperatures used to make these two types of pottery also differ. Earthenware is fired at approximately 1,100-1,200°C, whereas porcelain is fired at approximately 1,300°C, that is to say porcelain is generally fired at a higher temperature. The difference in information that can be conveyed to people through the five senses is due to the differences in the elements of the base material. In other words, different natural materials convey different messages.

　叩くと陶器は鈍い音が、磁器は金属音の冴えた音がする。温かなお茶を入れたときも、陶器はじんわりゆっくりと温かさが伝わってくるのに対して、磁器のほうは直に温度が手に伝わる。また、陶器は表面に小さな孔があいているから、抹茶など色素が濃いものを入れると徐々に素地に染みていき、長く使うことで色も変化して味わい深いものとなる。一方で磁器はガラスの器と同じように水分を通すことはない。

　このように両者は異なっており、それぞれの焼き上げる温度も異なる。陶器はおおよそ1100〜1200度、磁器は1300度前後と、一般的には磁器のほうが高い温度で焼かれる。五感を通じて、やきものから人に伝わる情報の差異は、素地となる自然な原料の違いである。つまり、自然から人へのメッセージが異なるのだ。

Shino Type Tea Bowl, Named "Wakamiya"
Mino ware / 16th-17th century /
MD 12.8cm / Kyushu National Museum

<ruby>志<rt>し</rt></ruby><ruby>野<rt>の</rt></ruby><ruby>茶<rt>ちゃ</rt></ruby><ruby>碗<rt>わん</rt></ruby>　<ruby>銘<rt>めい</rt></ruby>　<ruby>若<rt>わか</rt></ruby><ruby>宮<rt>みや</rt></ruby>／
美濃／16〜17世紀／
口径12.8㎝／九州国立博物館

Tea Bowl with Ridge on the Blade
Itaya Hazan / 1936 / MD 14.7cm /
Ibaraki Ceramic Art Museum

氷華磁鎬茶盌／
板谷波山／1963年
口径14.7㎝／茨城陶芸美術館

Forming

Differences Between Hand and Wheel Techniques

There are two typical methods for molding pottery: hand kneading with fingertips and making concentric circles using the potter's wheel.

The first representative technique is called "*rakuyaki*." In the late 16th century, Kyoto became the capital of *Chanoyu* (tea ceremony), and tea wares fired at low temperatures (700-800°C) were produced, including *rakuyaki*. The technique was developed by Raku Chojiro, the first generation of the Raku family which has been protecting and innovating the technique for 450 years, passing it down from generation to generation. The technique involves the use of soil inherited from previous generations in the Raku family, the soil is kneaded by hand to form the skeleton of a bowl and any excess is scraped off with a spatula. ChoJiro also created an asymmetrical fluctuation tea bowl with the inscription "*Omokage* (Remembrance)" (p. 26).

成形——手づくねとろくろの違い

　やきものの成形の代表的なものに、人の指先でこねてつくる手づくねという手法と、ろくろを使って同心円状のものをつくる手法がある。

　前者の代表は、楽焼の茶碗だ。16世紀後半の桃山時代、京都では茶の湯が隆盛し、楽焼をはじめ低火度（700〜800度）焼成のやきものが焼かれるようになる。初代長次郎から始まる樂家は、450年間一子相伝で技の伝統を守り革新している。その技は代々樂家に伝わる土を使い、手づくねでその土を締めながら立ち上げて茶碗の骨格をつくり、余分な土をへらで削り取っていくものだ。手づくねであるために彫刻のような造形も可能であり、長次郎もまた銘「面影」（p.26）のようにアンシンメトリーなゆらぎの茶碗を創造した。

　後者のろくろは回転盤のひとつで、木工や金工で円形にするのにも用いられるが、

The second technique uses the potter's wheel, a type of turntable also used to make circles in wood and metalwork, but the wheel used for pottery is generally a single disc turned by hand. Other types of wheels are used by sitting on a chair and are rotated by a kick with the foot, and some are electric.

In the mid-17th century, Nonomura Ninsei built a kiln near the entrance to the Omuro Ninna-ji temple in northwestern Kyoto, where he produced elegant tea ware (p. 27). The distortion-free symmetry of his molding technique using the potter's wheel is utterly terrific. Unlike paintings on flat surfaces, paintings on pottery can be seen from any of the three dimensions and require different techniques. Ninsei added red to blue, green and purple, and completed colored painting with a brush.

やきものをつくるためのろくろは1枚の円盤を手で回して使う。また椅子に座り、はずみ車を足で蹴って回転させるものや電動のものもある。野々村仁清は17世紀中ごろ京都の北西に位置する御室仁和寺（おむろにんなじ）門前で窯を開き、瀟洒（しょうしゃ）な茶器をつくり始めた（p.27）。ろくろを使ったゆがみのないシンメトリーの成形がみごとである。平面の絵とは異なり、やきものに描かれる絵は立体のいずれからも見られるものであり、異なった技が必要となる。仁清は青や緑、紫に赤を加えて、筆を使い色絵陶を完成させた。

Black Raku Tea Bowl, Named "*Omokage*"
Chojiro I / 16th century /
MD 9.9cm / Raku Museum

くろらくちゃわん めい おもかげ
黒樂茶碗　銘　面影
初代長次郎／16世紀／
口径9.9cm／樂美術館

Tea Bowl with Overglaze Enamel Design of Plum Blossoms
Nonomura Ninsei / 1936 /
MD 12.3cm / Tokyo National Museum

<ruby>色<rt>いろ</rt></ruby><ruby>絵<rt>え</rt></ruby><ruby>梅<rt>ばい</rt></ruby><ruby>花<rt>か</rt></ruby><ruby>文<rt>もん</rt></ruby><ruby>茶<rt>ちゃ</rt></ruby><ruby>碗<rt>わん</rt></ruby>
色絵梅花文茶碗
野々村仁清／17世紀／
口径 12.3cm ／東京国立博物館

Source: ColBase(https://colbase.nich.go.jp)　27

Chato (Tea Pottery)

The pottery used in *Chanoyu* is called "*chato* (tea pottery)." At the end of the 16th century, master of *Chanoyu* Sen no Rikyu (p. 121) created the concept of "*wabi*," which promoted a new sense of value for *chato*. Until then, the pottery that was imported from China was considered to be the best. But with the improvement of the pottery technology in Japan, the beauty of domestic pottery was to be polished by master of *Chanoyu*. In the world of *Chanoyu*, it has long been said that tea bowls are ranked or rated as "*Ichi Raku Ni Hagi San Karatsu* (1st: Raku ware, 2nd: Hagi ware, 3rd: Karatsu ware)." In the tea ceremony, the tools used are numerous and varied. It is no exaggeration to say that *Kogei* (Japanese art of crafts) have nurtured beauty together with the way of tea. Tea pottery was chosen by the master of *Chanoyu* to perform the best hospitality in the tea ceremony, and sometimes the pottery was created by potters and craftsmen to embody the wishes of master of *Chanoyu*. In 1906, *The Book of Tea* by Okakura Tenshin conveyed the beauty of the way of tea to the world.

茶陶

　　茶の湯で使われるやきものを「茶陶」と言う。16世紀の末、千利休 (p.121) が茶陶に新しい価値観である「侘（わ）び」という概念を創出した。侘び茶が隆盛すると、それまでは中国伝来のものが最上とされていたが、国内でのやきものの技術の向上とも相まって、茶人により国内のやきものの美が磨かれることとなった。特に楽焼、萩焼、唐津焼の茶碗は「一楽二萩三唐津」と称された。茶の湯では多くのまた多彩な道具が用いられる。日本の工芸は茶の湯とともに美を育んできたといっても過言ではないだろう。「茶陶」は茶人が最高のもてなしを茶事で行うために選んだもので、時には陶芸家や職人に茶人の想いを具現化するために、創作させたやきものもある。1906年の岡倉天心の著『The Book of Tea』は、茶の湯の美を世界に伝えた。

Chapter 2

Decoration

第二章

装飾

Various Decoration Methods

With the development of the kiln, clay could continue to be fired for extended periods of time at temperatures as high as 1,000°C. The ashes from burning fuel would fall on the surface of the soil and combine with the silicic acid in it to form a thick layer of glassy material. As a result of the ash flowing down the surface, a natural pattern was created. When people realized that this natural glassy material that coated the surface of pottery not only colored it and made it glossy, but also strengthened it and made it waterproof, they started to search for materials and, through trial and error, discovered various techniques based on their experience. Gradually, it was found that melting the ash of straw and rice husks and firing them on the base material produces a white or milky white glaze. People also came to realize that when the base is covered with white mud and fired, it looks as if the soil is wearing white makeup. With the creation of white pottery, people learned how to freely and diversely decorate these works using various techniques such as drawing pictures on them and painting them, carving the surface of the base material by scraping it, using a different-colored soil on the carved parts, etc.

多彩な装飾法

　窯が発達して、1000度以上の高温のなかで長く焚き続けられるようになると、燃料の灰が素地表面に降りつもり、土肌を覆い、土に含まれている成分と混ざり合って厚いガラス質の層になって表面を流れ、自然の文様が出来上がった。これを自然釉といい、やきものに光沢と色を与え、漏水や浸水を防止し、強固にするものであることを知ると、人々は素材を探し、何度も試して経験からさまざまな技法を見つけ出していく。藁（わら）やもみ殻の灰を溶かして素地にかけて焼くと白や乳白色になることや、白い泥で素地を覆って焼くとまるで化粧のように見た目が白くなることを発見していく。そして白いやきものができるようになると、そこに絵を描くようになったり、素地の表面を削ったり、彫ったところに違う色の土を入れたりなど、自由でさまざまな装飾が可能となったのだ。

Ash Glaze

The most ancient glaze and the basis for all kinds of glazes. The pale and transparent blue of celadon was also discovered by studying the ash glaze. Trees with low iron content such as *isunoki* and *keyaki* are used to obtain a pale yellowish-green, while rice straw and chaff are used to obtain a pale milky white.

Horizontal Jar with Ash Glaze   Sanage ware / 9th century / H 13.6cm, BD 20.0cm / Aichi Prefectural Ceramic Museum

灰釉
^{かいゆう}

　最も古い釉薬で、あらゆる釉の基本ともなるもの。青磁の淡い透明感のある青も灰釉が研究されたものだ。淡い黄緑色の場合は、イスノキや欅（けやき）など鉄分の少ない樹木を用いり、淡い乳白色の場合は稲藁やもみ殻が使われている。

灰釉鳥形平瓶　猿投／９世紀／高 13.6㎝　胴径 20.0㎝／愛知県陶磁美術館

Green Glaze

The history of the bright green glaze can be traced back to the 2nd century BC. The green glaze gained popularity during Roman times in the West and China's Han Dynasty in the East. In Japan, Oribe ware with a bold green design became popular in the 16th century.

Incense Burner with Lion-shaped Knob, Oribe Type Mino ware / 1612 / H 20.9cm / Tokyo National Museum

_{りょくゆう}
緑釉

　鮮やかな緑色の釉薬の歴史は紀元前2世紀にまでさかのぼれる。西洋ではローマ、東洋では中国の漢の時代に流行が見られる。日本では16世紀に緑を大胆に意匠した織部焼が流行する。

織部獅子鈕香炉　美濃／1612年／総高20.9cm／東京国立博物館

Straw Ash Glaze

The whiteness seen in Hagi ware is mainly due to the use of a glaze made of straw ash, which is produced by burning rice straw. The whiteness of the glaze has the warmth of freshly cooked rice, which may be a result of the raw materials used.

Tea Bowl with Notched Foot, Hagi ware, Oni-Hagi Type   Miwa Jusetsu (Kyusetsu XI) / 2003 / MD 16.5cm / Agency for Cultural Affairs, Government of Japan

藁灰釉
<small>わらばいゆう</small>

　萩焼などに見られる白さは、稲藁を燃やしてできる藁灰を主原料とした釉薬が使われている。原料に由来してか、その白さには炊き立てご飯のような温かみがある。

鬼萩割高台茶碗 <small>おにはぎわりこうだいちゃわん</small>　三輪壽雪（11代休雪）／2003年／口径16.5cm／文化庁

Kohiki

Kohiki is a technique of covering a blackish base material containing extra iron with white decorative soil and applying a transparent glaze before firing. As the decorative soil is different from the base material in shrinkage rate, it develops crackles on the surface called "*kan'nyu.*"

Sake Bottle with Glazed on White Slip　Hagi ware / 17th-18th century / H 15cm / The Museum Yamato Bunkakan

粉引

　　粉引は土の鉄分が多く黒っぽい素地を白い色の化粧土で覆い、透明釉をかけて焼く技法。化粧土は素地と収縮率が異なるためひび（貫入）が入り景色となる。

萩粉引徳利　萩／17〜18世紀／高15cm／大和文華館

Hakeme

Hakeme is a technique of applying white decorative soil on the base material with a brush and firing it with a transparent glaze. It is called *hakeme* technique because the patterns are created by brush strokes. Depending on the brush type, decorative soil concentration and usage, this technique allows various and free expression. Type of Korean tea bowl.

Tea Bowl with Brushed Pattern Ishiguro Munemaro / 1963 / H 5.4cm, MD 15.2cm / Ishikawa Prefectural Museum of Art

刷毛目

素地に白い化粧土を刷毛で塗り、透釉薬をかけて焼く技法。刷毛跡で模様ができるため刷毛目と呼ばれる。刷毛の種類や化粧土の濃度、また刷毛の使い方次第で多様で自由な表現できる。高麗茶碗を祖にもつ。

刷毛目平茶碗 石黒宗麿／1963年／高5.4cm 口径15.2cm／石川県立美術館

Sabi-e

A technique of drawing on an unglazed base material with paints and glazes containing iron oxide (a rusty component of iron) such as *bengara* (red iron oxide) or iron sand. Painting is done before applying a transparent glaze. After firing, the color of the painting turns from black to reddish brown; the subdued color produces a serene picture.

Large Dish with Iron Glaze Design of Reed   Karatsu ware /
16th-17th century / D 41.8cm / Kyushu National Museum

Sometsuke

Sometsuke is a technique of painting on a white base material (generally porcelain), with *gosu* (cobalt oxide) pigment. The patterns drawn with a brush in indigo blue or blue-purple color on a white background stand out beautifully.

Large Tripod Dish with Underglaze Cobalt-blue Design of Herons
Nabeshima official kiln / Important Cultural Property / 1690-1710s / D 28.0cm / The Kyushu Ceramic Museum

染付

　下絵の一種。白色の素地に、呉須（酸化コバルト）の顔料で絵を描く技法。藍青色（らんせいしょく）や青紫色を呈して、白地に筆で描かれた文様が美しく浮かび上がる。

染付鷺文三足皿　鍋島藩窯／重文／1690〜1710年代／径28.0cm／
佐賀県立九州陶磁文化館

Iro-e

The technique of applying transparent glaze to an unglazed base material and firing it at a high temperature, painting it with overglaze colors and then firing it again at a low temperature of about 800°C. It is also called "*uwa-e* (overglaze painting)." Works using this technique are also known as "*iro-e*."

Jar for Tea Leaves with Overglaze Polychrome Enamel Design of Moon and Plum Blossoms Studio of Ninsei / Important Cultural Property / 17th century / H 29.9cm / Tokyo National Museum

色絵

素焼きした素地に透明釉をかけ高温で焼成した後に、赤・緑・黄・紫・青などの上絵具で彩色して、約800度の低い温度でもう一度焼いて仕上げる技法。釉薬の上から描くので「上絵」とも呼ばれる。この技法を使った作品も色絵と呼ぶ。
色絵月梅図茶壺 野々村仁清／重文／17世紀／高29.9cm／東京国立博物館

Kinrande

Kinrande is a technique of decorating white porcelain overglazed with paints such as red, green, yellow, purple, and blue at low temperatures by adding gold or silver paint. In some cases, gilded white porcelain is not fired over. Works using this technique are called *kinrande* in Japan, because this decoration resembles the gold brocade of textiles.

Large Dish with Overglaze Polychrome Enamel Design of Lady with Parasol
Arita ware / 1700-1740s / The Kyushu Ceramic Museum

金襴手

　赤・緑・黄・紫・青などの絵具で上絵付した白磁に、金彩、銀彩を加えて低火度で焼き付ける技法。金箔を張り付けた場合は焼き付けない場合もある。この技法を使った作品も金襴手と呼ぶ。織物の金襴に似ているので日本では金襴手と呼ばれた。

色絵傘美人文大皿　有田／1700～1740年代／佐賀県立九州陶磁文化館

Zogan (Inlay)

Zogan is a decorative technique in which the surface of the base material is engraved with lines or seals, and inlaying the engraved surface with clay of a different color from the base material. In ceramic art the inlay is applied while the base material is half-dry; when it dries, colored soil is leveled off with a spatula and adhered, and then the entire piece is glazed and fired.

Water Jar with White Slip Inlaid Design of Bamboo   Yatsushiro ware / 18th-19th century / The Kyushu Ceramic Museum

象嵌

　素地の表面に線刻、印刻などを施し、彫ったところに素地とは色が異なる粘土を嵌（は）め込む装飾の技法。陶芸では素地が生乾きの状態で象嵌を施し、乾いたら色土をへらなどで均らして密着させ、全体に釉薬をかけて焼く。

ぞうがんたけもんひらみずさし
象嵌竹文平水指　八代／18世紀後半〜19世紀／佐賀県立九州陶磁文化館

Tobikan'na

A formed half-dried base material or base material dried after applying decorative soil is placed on the potter's wheel. When an elastic plane or spatula is applied to the surface of the base material and the potter's wheel is rotated, narrow cuts are instantly formed at equal intervals. The dashed line pattern and its technique are called "*tobikan'na*."

Large Dish   Onta ware /
D 54.0cm / Oita Prefectural Art Museum

飛び鉋

　成形した生乾きの素地、または化粧土をかけた後に乾燥させた素地をろくろに置く。素地の表面に弾力性のある鉋やへらをあて、ろくろを回転させると、表面に等しい間隔で狭い切れ目が入る。この破線状の文様とその技法を「飛び鉋」と呼ぶ。

飛び鉋大皿　小鹿田／径54.0㎝／大分県立美術館

Icchin (Slipware)

The decorative technique of forming a line pattern by squeezing slurry and glaze out of a tool called "*icchin*" and heaping it up. In the West, this technique is known as slipware.

Vase with Yellow Glazed design of a Flower and a Hand   Kawai Kanjiro / 1950 / H 22.0cm, MD 4.7cm / Aichi Prefectural Ceramic Museum

イッチン（筒描き）

イッチンという道具に泥漿（でいしょう）や釉薬を入れて絞り出し、盛り上げて線文を表す装飾の技法もイッチンと呼ばれる。西洋ではこの技法をスリップウェアという。

黄釉筒描花と手文扁壺   河井寛次郎／1950年／高22.0cm　口径4.7cm／愛知県陶磁美術館

The Mingei Movement

Yanagi Soyetsu, a philosopher, found aesthetic value in everyday objects, which had not previously been seen as objects of beauty, and developed a cultural and crafts movement, called the *Mingei* (folk art) movement. In 1925, Yanagi Soyetsu, along with potters Hamada Shoji and Kawai Kanjiro, named the folk arts that were made by unknown craftsmen and used by the people in their daily lives. In 1926, potter Tomimoto Kenkichi (p. 121) agreed with the movement's principles, and Yanagi started the *Mingei* movement. Yanagi and the others investigated crafts, collected objects held exhibitions. In 1931, they also launched the magazine *Kogei* as a bulletin for the *Mingei* movement. In 1936, the Japan Folk Crafts Museum was also established in Komaba, Tokyo, as a base for the popularization of *Mingei*'s concept of beauty and the *Mingei* movement. This movement has contributed to the revitalization of the indigenous and traditional techniques of each region.

民藝運動

　思想家である柳宗悦はそれまで美の対象とされてこなかった民衆の暮らしに息づく日常品に、美的価値を見いだし文化・造形運動を展開した。この運動を民藝運動という。1925年柳宗悦は陶芸家濱田庄司や河井寛次郎らとともに、無名の職人達がつくり、民衆が暮らしで用いた民衆的工芸品を「民藝」と名付けた。1926年には陶芸家の富本健吉 (p.121) もこの運動に賛同し、柳は民藝運動を始動させる。柳らは民芸品を調査・蒐集し公開するために展覧会を催し、1931年には民藝運動の機関紙として雑誌『工藝』も創刊した。1936年には「民藝」の美の概念の普及と民藝運動の本拠として東京・駒場に日本民藝館も設立した。民藝運動により各地の土着的・伝統的な技術が復興した。

Chapter 3

Pottery
in
Western Japan

第三章

やきものめぐりの旅
西日本編

Arita Ware
(Saga Prefecture)

The town of Arita is located in a valley in western Saga Prefecture, and the porcelain made in the area is called Arita ware. Until modern times, it was called Imari ware, since it was transported by boat from Imari Port. This porcelain, which fascinated royalty and aristocracy in Europe, was called IMARI and influenced Western porcelain. At the beginning of the 17th century, ceramic stones were found to be the raw material for porcelain and Arita became known as the town where porcelain was made for the first time in Japan. You can stroll along the cobblestone pavement of Izumiyama Quarry, which was once a potter's stone mining site, and the Tombai Wall Alleys, made of abandoned bricks and broken dishes, as if to mark the history of the site. Color-painted porcelain representative of Imari-Arita ware can be broadly divided into three styles: Kakiemon, Ko-Imari, and Iro-Nabeshima style. The Kakiemon style features the Japanese unique beauty of margins, with red, green, yellow, and indigo overpainting on a milky-white base material. The Ko-imari style is characterized by its gorgeous gold brocade that impressed people in Europe. The Iro-Nabeshima style, which is traditionally used as a gift that cannot be seen by ordinary people, retains to the present day its exceptional quality.

有田焼（佐賀県）

　有田町は佐賀県西部の谷あいにあり、その周辺でつくられる磁器を有田焼と呼ぶ。近代までは伊万里港から船で輸送されたため伊万里焼と呼ばれた。欧州の王侯貴族を魅了したこの磁器はIMARIと呼ばれ西洋の磁器にも影響を与えた。17世紀初めに磁器の原料となる陶石が見つかり、日本で初めて磁器がつくられるようになった有田の町は、その歴史を刻むように、陶石の採掘場であった泉山磁石場や、廃煉瓦

**Large Dish in Kraak Style with Underglaze
Cobalt-blue Design of Phoenix**
Imari ware / 1690-1710s / The Kyushu Ceramic Museum

や壊れた皿でできたトンバイ塀に石畳と風情ある小道を散策できる。伊万里・有田焼
を代表する色絵磁器は、柿右衛門様式、古伊万里様式、色鍋島に大別される。柿
右衛門様式は乳白色の濁手（にごしで）の素地に、赤、緑、黄、藍で上絵付し素地を
活かす日本独特の余白の美が魅力的だ。古伊万里様式は欧州の人々を圧倒させた
華麗な金襴手が特徴だ。色鍋島は庶民が目にすることもできない献上用だった歴史
から厳格な品質が今も守られ気品が香る。

Deep Bowl with Overglaze Enamel Design of Flower and Bird
Kakiemon Type / Important Cultural Property / 17th century
MD 30.3cm / Tokyo National Museum

**Porcelain Bowl with
Overglaze Enamel Design of
the Daoist Immortal Qin Gao**
Imari ware /
17th-18th century /
MD 22.8cm /
Tokyo National Museum

色絵花鳥文大鉢
伊万里 (柿右衛門様式) ／重文／17世紀／
口径30.3cm ／東京国立博物館
色絵琴高仙人図鉢
伊万里／17〜18世紀／
口径22.8cm ／東京国立博物館

Dish with Overglaze Polychrome Enamel Design of Cherry Blossoms
Nabeshima official kiln / 1700-1720s / MD 20.3cm /
The Kyushu Ceramic Museum

いろえおうじゅもんさら
色絵桜樹文皿
鍋島藩窯／1700〜1720年代／
口径20.3cm／佐賀県立九州陶磁文化館

Satsuma Ware
(Kagoshima Prefecture)

Kagoshima Prefecture is located at the southernmost part of Kyushu, and the main island of Okinawa is at a short distance of approximately 20 kilometers from the southern island of Yoron. They have many things in common, such as "*kara-kara*" the name used to refer to sake decanters. The origin of Satsuma ware dates back to 1598, when a potter from Korea opened a kiln. Satsuma ware is roughly divided into Shiromon and Kuromon. Shiromon pottery is characterized by the white skin-like porcelain and a gorgeous pattern of *kinrande* or gold brocade. When white soil of Korean origin was discovered in this area, pottery with fine crackles on the surface covered with a transparent glaze to enhance its whiteness was produced. At first, only a limited number of people were allowed to see this high-quality pottery. Shiromon ware, which was called SATSUMA at the Paris Expo in 1867, crossed the sea when Japan opened its borders and fascinated people in Europe. On the other hand, in Satsuma there are many active volcanoes and iron-rich soil can be found. Kuromon is made of this clay that turns black when fired at high temperatures and glazed with black or dark brown. Due to their strength and solidness, it is popular not only for daily use but also as tea pottery.

色絵秋草図茶碗
薩摩／19世紀中頃／
口径9.8cm／東京国立博物館

Tea Bowl with Overglaze Enamel Design of Autumn Grasses
Satsuma ware / ca. Mid 19th century /
MD 9.8cm / Tokyo National Museum

に細かな貫入があるやきものができる。当初は限られた層の者しか見ることも許されない高級陶器だった。日本が開国され海を渡った白もんは1867年のパリ万博でSATSUMAと呼ばれ欧州の人々を魅了した。また、薩摩は活火山が多い土地で鉄分が豊富な土がとれる。黒もんは焼けると黒くなるこの陶土を使い黒釉や蕎麦釉をかけ高温で焼いたもの。頑丈さと重厚さをもつ器は日常だけでなく茶陶としても好まれる。

Jar with Dark-brown Glaze and Dragon Applique Design
Satsuma ware / Second half of 17th century-18th century /
The Kyushu Ceramic Museum

Kilns in Western Japan

⑥ ⑪ ⑨ ⑦ ③ ① ④ ⑧ ⑩ ② ⑤

Karatsu Ware
(Saga Prefecture)

Named after the Japanese words *Kara* (meaning China and Korea) and *Tsu* (port), the town of Karatsu, facing the Genkai Sea, has prospered since ancient times as a gateway to the continent. Karatsu ware, which takes its name from the place, is attractive for its rough soil flavor, and characterized by the various techniques introduced from Korea. Chosen Karatsu refers to ware with blackish-brown and milky-white glazes applied separately. The blackish-brown iron glaze is covered with whitish straw-ash glaze, and the flow of the glazes, blended colors, and discoloration of the ware (see *yohen*, p. 121) can be appreciated. The main feature of Madara Karatsu ware is the pattern of natural spots in blue and black, where the iron content of the base material is melted in the milky-white straw-ash colored glaze. E-Karatsu, a painting of flowers and birds drawn using iron pigments with subdued colors, is said to be the earliest pottery painting in Japan. The clockwise *kerokuro* (kicking potter's wheel) and *noborigama* (climbing kiln), which originated in Korea, still exist.

唐津焼 (佐賀県)

　玄関灘に面した港町・唐津は、中国や朝鮮を意味する唐と、船着き場を意味する津という名のとおり、大陸への玄関口として栄えた。唐津焼は、ざっくりとした荒い土の味わいが魅力的な陶器で、朝鮮から伝わった技が多種あることが特徴だ。朝鮮唐津は黒褐色と乳白色の釉薬が掛け分けられたもの。黒っぽい褐色となる鉄釉に、白っぽい色がでる藁灰釉をかけ、その流れ具合や溶け合った色、窯変 (p.121) を楽しむ。斑 (まだら) 唐津は藁灰釉が醸す乳白色に素地の鉄分が熔けた青や黒の自然にできたまだらな点の文様が見どころだ。草花や鳥を鉄絵で描いた落ち着いた色合いの絵唐津は日本で初めての絵付けともいわれている。町には、朝鮮を祖とする時計回りの蹴ろくろ、登り窯などが今も息づく。

Jar with Underglaze Iron-brown Design of Bush Clover
Karatsu ware / 1590-1610s / The Kyushu Ceramic Museum

Water Jar,
Korean Karatsu Type
Karatsu ware / 17th century /
H 15.8cm, MD 9.1cm /
Kyushu National Museum

鉄絵萩文壺
唐津／1590〜1610年代／
佐賀県立九州陶磁文化館
朝鮮唐津水指
唐津／17世紀／
高15.8cm　口径9.1cm／九州国立博物館

Source: ColBase(https://colbase.nich.go.jp)　55

Onta Ware
(Oita Prefecture)

Onta ware has been produced for over 300 years, and its ceramic techniques have been secretly passed down from parent to child. Although the soil of this area is relatively poor, a refining technique known as "*suihi*" makes it suitable for pottery by drying dug soil, crushing it into small pieces over a period of three weeks with a water-powered millstone, mixing it with water, and then filtering it to remove pebbles. This method involves the process of repeatedly refining muddy water, draining it in a filter tank, and drying the polished clay. It is extremely time-consuming and laborious. Once ready, the clay is shaped using a kicking potter's wheel and decorated using techniques such as consecutive scratches or *tobikan'na*, brush strokes or *hakeme* and combed lines or *kushigaki* (p. 122); subsequently, it is glazed with undertone colors like black and green, and finally, fired in a climbing kiln. In 1931, Yanagi Soyetsu praised the sublime beauty of Onta ware in his book *Hita no Sarayama*. Later, Bernard Leach (p. 122) visited his residence to work on ceramics, which eventually made this simple, heartwarming, and practical pottery internationally well-known.

小鹿田焼（大分県）

　小鹿田焼は、300年以上にわたり一子相伝で受け継がれている。小鹿田の陶土はむしろ悪かった。それでも、ここで採れる土を乾かし、流れる川の水力を使った唐臼で3週間かけて細かく砕き、水を加えてかき混ぜ、小石などを取り除く「水簸（すいひ）」という精製方法で、泥水を何度も濾し、濾過槽で水をぬいて乾燥させ、陶土をつくり続けている。手間暇かかる仕事である。その陶土を蹴ろくろで成形し、飛び鉋、刷毛目、櫛描き（p.122）などの技法を使って装飾し、黒や緑などの落ち着いた色の釉薬をかけ、登り窯で本焼きする。1931年柳宗悦が著書『日田の皿山』で小鹿田焼を賞賛。その後バーナード・リーチ（p.122）がこの地で作陶し、素朴で温かな日常雑器を世に知らしめることとなった。

Ewer with Trailed Copper-green on Brown Glaze and White Slip
Onta ware / 19th-20th century /
The Kyushu Ceramic Museum

Sake Bottle
Onta ware /
ca. Late 19th century-Early 20th
century / H 30.0cm /
Oita Prefectural Art Museum

ながしがけゆうすいちゅう
流掛釉水注
小鹿田／19〜20世紀／
佐賀県立九州陶磁文化館
つつがもんみちゆきとくり
筒描き文道行徳利
小鹿田／19世紀後半〜20世紀前半頃／
高30.0cm／大分県立美術館

Tsuboya Ware

(Okinawa Prefecture)

Okinawa, which includes the westernmost and southernmost points of Japan, was once an independent kingdom called Ryukyu. When walking along Tsuboya and Yachimun Street from Sakurazaka in Naha, a pleasant breeze flows as if experiencing the hustle and bustle of an international street. The area, that miraculously escaped the ravages of war, is lined with unique studios and pottery shops with climbing kilns, recognized as cultural property. In Okinawa dialect, "*yachimun*" means pottery and "*tsuboya*" means kiln. Tsuboya ware, which has a history of about 300 years, can be broadly divided into two types of pottery: Arayachi (unglazed) and Joyachi (glazed). Arayachi pottery has a reddish-brown color with the strength and warmth created by the high-quality, unique Okinawan clay from which sake and water jars are mainly made. Joyachi pottery is made of red-soil as a base material covered with the glaze unique to Tsuboya. The bold and powerful patterns reflecting the mixed Ryukyu culture of Japan, China, and Southeast Asia are painted with unique fish and plants, and some patterns, such as *kakiotoshi* and *tobikan'na*, exhibit the base material of red soil. The sake decanters, called "*kara-kara*", are also attractive.

壺屋焼（沖縄県）

　沖縄は、かつて琉球という独立した王国だった。那覇の桜坂から壺屋やちむん通りは、戦禍を奇跡的に免れた界隈で、文化財の登り窯に個性豊かな工房や陶器店が並ぶ。沖縄の言葉で壺屋は窯場を、やちむんはやきものを意味する。約300年の歴史をもつ壺屋焼は、焼締めの荒焼（あらやち）と釉薬をかけた上焼（じょうやち）に大別される。荒焼は沖縄独特の良質の陶土が醸す力強さや温かみがある赤褐色をしており、主に大きな酒甕（さかがめ）や水甕がつくられている。上焼は赤土の素地に壺屋独特の釉薬がかけられたもの。日本、中国、東南アジアが混交した琉球文化を映した大胆で迫力ある絵柄には、ここにしかない魚や植物が描かれ、掻き落とし、飛び鉋など赤土の素地を見せた文様も見られる。カラカラと呼ばれる酒器も楽しい。

Jar with Overglaze Polychrome Enamel Design of Fish
Kinjo Jiro / ca. 1960-65 / H 24.7cm, D 30.5cm /
Agency for Cultural Affairs, Government of Japan

Wine Bottle with Spout
Tsuboya ware /
19th century / H 10.0cm /
Tokyo National Museum

59

Bizen Ware

(Okayama Prefecture)

The origin of Bizen ware is believed to be Sue pottery brought in from the Korean Peninsula in the 5th century and ceramic utensils for daily use began to be produced approximately a thousand years ago. As *Chanoyu* (tea ceremony) grew in popularity after the latter half of the 16th century, Bizen ware was in fashion among masters of *Chanoyu*. Bizen ceramics adopted the *yakishime* technique to fire the pottery without using glaze, and is known for its attractive earthy color, natural designs, as well as for the Hidasuki, Goma, Tamadare, and Sangiri patterns. In the process of making Bizen ware, rice field clay, known as "*hiyose*," is dried and soaked in water for elutriation. The sorted clay is then placed in a bowl until it is suitably hard, and subsequently kneaded well to ensure a favorable condition for usage. As Bizen ware does not apply glaze, ensuring a high-quality clay is of utmost importance for artisans who, therefore, devote plenty of effort to making the finest clay. The worked clay is shaped using techniques like coil-building of long clay strings (see *himotsukuri* p. 122) or on the potter's wheel, and baked in a climbing kiln after drying. The kiln filling is essential because scenery on the surface differs depending on when the pottery is placed in the climbing kiln and which direction it faces.

備前焼（岡山県）

　備前焼は、5世紀に朝鮮半島から伝わった須恵器に起源をもち、今からおよそ1000年前には生活用のやきものもつくられるようになった。16世紀後半から茶の湯において侘び茶が好まれると、備前焼が茶人のあいだで流行するようになった。備前焼は釉薬を使わない「焼締め」で土色や自然にできた文様、緋襷（ひだすき）、胡麻、玉だれ、桟切（さんぎり）など景色が楽しめる。「干寄（ひよせ）」と呼ばれる田土を乾燥さ

Large Jar with Fire Marks
Bizen ware / 16th-17th century /
H 40.5cm / Tokyo National Museum

せ、水につけ、鉢に盛り、ほどよい硬さになると、今度はよく揉んで土づくりをする。釉薬を使わない焼締めでは、土づくりが非常に大切で、作り手は独自の土づくりに専念する。紐つくり（p.122）やろくろで成形し、乾燥させた後、登り窯で焼成する。登り窯のどこに置くか、どの向きに置くかで現れる景色も異なるため、窯詰めが肝だという。

Wastewater Receptacle in the Shape of a Mochi Rice Cake
Bizen ware / Beginning of 17th century / H 10.1cm, BD 16.9cm /
Okayama Prefectural Museum of Art

び ぜんかさねもちがたけんすい
備前重餅形建水
備前／17世紀初頭／高10.1cm　胴径16.9cm
岡山県立美術館

Tea Caddy Named "Nio"
Bizen ware / 16th-17th century /
Tokyo National Museum

かたつまちゃいれ めい に おう
肩衝茶入 銘 二王
備前／16～17世紀／
東京国立博物館

Source: ColBase(https://colbase.nich.go.jp) 63

Hagi Ware
(Yamaguchi Prefecture)

Hagi ware originated approximately 400 years ago. With the proliferation of *Chanoyu*, Hagi ware was very popular as a lineage of Korean ceramic teacups amongst masters of *Chanoyu*. Hagi, therefore, flourished as an area that produced tea utensils. The base clay of Hagi ware is made mainly with off-white Daido soil that is added to white Mitake soil and dark-red Mishima soil. Hagi ware can be identified by its soft and plump shape with an earthy texture. Artisans seek their own perfect composition of different soils to create the refined earthy color of the clay. As for its decoration, firewood ash glaze is primarily used to induce a transparent color, and straw-ash glaze for a milky-white shade. To generate the loquat color of earthy texture, the artisans examine the best composition of those glazes. Also, the shaped clay of Hagi ware is normally heated in a climbing kiln and the pottery is loosely compacted for a soft texture due to which green tea easily penetrates a piece through the fine web of crackles, gradually changing the surface color over time. This is the reason why Hagi ware is described as "seven disguises."

萩焼（山口県）

　およそ400年前、茶の湯の隆盛とともに、萩焼は高麗茶碗の系譜茶碗として、茶人のあいだで愛され、茶陶の産地として栄えるようになった。この地で産出される灰白色の大道（だいどう）土を基本に、白色の金峯（みたけ）土や、赤黒色の見島（みしま）土を加えて素地をつくる。萩焼は柔らかくふっくらした土味が重要で、作り手は自身がめざす土味をだすために土の配合を研究する。釉薬は主に透明となる土灰釉、乳

Hagi Ware Tea Bowl in the Shape of a Brush Washer
Miwa Kyuwa (Kyusetsu X) / 1975 / MD 12.6cm /
Hagi Uragami Museum

白色となる藁灰釉を使うが、作り手は釉薬との関係で枇杷（びわ）色の土味をどのように醸すかに切磋琢磨し、独自の配合の釉薬をつくっている。この地では登り窯で焼成することが多く、焼き締まりがゆるく柔らかい土味が誕生した。見どころの貫入からは使うほどに抹茶が浸透し経年変化していく。「萩の七化け」と呼ばれる所以である。

Tobe Ware

(Ehime Prefecture)

Tobe in the Shikoku region has been blessed with good quality whetstones since the Nara period (701 to 784 AD), and its residents started to utilize scrap stones for porcelain at the end of the 18th century, which eventually developed into a successful so-called recycling industry in the region. In the 19th century, pottery stones were found in the Tobe River, which enabled the mass production of white porcelain with a relatively thick body and warm color. As it is durable enough not to break even if dropped, Tobe ware is suitable for export, and items such as the "Iyo Bowl" have gained popularity abroad. With its plump, round shape and abstract patterns of flowers depicted in soft indigo made from zaffer pigment combined with baked clay, Tobe ware reflected the mild climate of the Seto Inland Sea, and has been widely used as daily tableware. Yanagi Soyetsu, Bernard Leach, and Tomimoto Kenkichi visited Tobe and were inspired by the modern patterns of its products.

砥部焼 (愛媛県)

　四国地方にあり、8世紀頃から刃物を研ぐ砥石の産地であった砥部は、18世紀の終わりに砥石くずを磁器の原料に使うために人知を尽くして成功した、言わばリサイクル産業の地だ。19世紀に入ると砥部川で陶石が発見され、磁器としては厚手で温かみのある色の白磁が量産できるようになる。落としても割れにくい堅牢さをもつ磁器は輸出にも適しており「伊予ボール」として海外でも人気を博した。丸みを帯びたふく

Covered Jar with Blue Underglaze Design of Grape and Squirrel
Tobe ware / 19th century / H 24.8cm /
Aichi Prefectural Ceramic Museum

よかな形に、焼いた泥を加えた独自の呉須が醸し出す柔らかな藍色が特徴。また、描かれた抽象的な草花の文様は、瀬戸内の温暖な気候を映すように優しい雰囲気にあふれ、日常使いのテーブルウェアとして使われるようになった。柳宗悦、バーナード・リーチ、富本憲吉も訪れ、影響を与えた地の器だけに、モダンな文様は飽きがこない。

Chapter 4

Pottery
in Kyoto
and
Surroundings

第四章

やきものめぐりの旅
京都とその周辺

Kyo Ware
(Kyoto Prefecture)

Pottery often reflects the history and characteristics of a place. Kyo ware are no exception, embodying Kyoto's unique tradition and traits. However, it is not uncommon to hear that Kyo ware have no distinctive features. Why is that? In Kyoto, Japan's capital city for more than a thousand years, potters have always been demanded by the powers that be to make the most advanced and highest quality pottery. For this reason, many of Kyoto's popular potters were considered the greatest potters of their time, including Chojiro of Raku family, Hon'ami Koetsu (p. 123), Nonomura Ninsei, Ogata Kenzan (p. 123), Nin'ami Dohachi (p. 123), Kawai Kanjiro, and Tomimoto Kenkichi. In fact, it is precisely because Kyoto, as a large city, was neither rich in clay nor suitable for firing in pit kilns or climbing kilns that the Kyo ware flourished garnering additional value to the pottery. Further, its cultural environment of being the center of *Chanoyu* and *Senchado* (tea ceremony with leaf tea) forced Kyoto to produce sophisticated tea utensils and tableware that nicely fit into people's hands.

京焼（京都府）

　土地の歴史や特徴を映すやきものがある。京焼もまた、京都という土地の歴史と特徴を映している。よく京焼には特徴がないといわれる。それはなぜか。1000年ものあいだ日本の都だった京都では、陶芸家はつねに時の権力者らから流行の最先端で最高級のやきものづくりを要求され続けてきたという背景がある。だからこそ、樂家初代長次郎、本阿弥光悦（p.123）、野々村仁清、尾形乾山（p.123）、仁阿弥道八

Black Raku Tea Bowl, Named "Shigure"
Hon'ami Koetsu / 17th century /
MD 12.4cm / Nagoya City Museum

（p.123）、河井寛次郎、富本憲吉など、各時代の寵児（ちょうじ）となる陶芸家を生み出したのだろう。自然に恵まれた陶土があったわけでもなければ、穴窯や登り窯で焼くには不便な土地柄で、大都会ならではの、付加価値をつけることで興隆してきたのだ。そして、茶の湯や煎茶の流行の中心地でもあった京都では、茶器や料理の器の使い手にも、研ぎ澄まされた洗練が求められた。

Incense Burner Shape of Pheasant Decorated with Overglaze Enamels
Nonomura Ninsei / National Treasure / 17th century /
H 18.1cm, D 48.3cm / Ishikawa Prefectural Museum of Art

色絵雉香炉
<ruby>色<rt>いろ</rt>絵<rt>え</rt>雉<rt>きじ</rt>香<rt>こう</rt>炉<rt>ろ</rt></ruby>
野々村仁清／国宝／17世紀／
高18.1cm　幅48.3cm／石川県立美術館

**Square Dish with Underglaze Iron Design
of Chinese Figure Watching Seagulls**
Ogata Korin and Kenzan / Important Cultural Property /
17th century / D 22.2cm / Tokyo National Museum

さびえかんおうずかくざら
銹絵観鷗図角皿
尾形光琳画、尾形乾山作／重文／17世紀／
径22.2cm／東京国立博物館

Sake Bottle with Overglaze Enamel Design of Bamboo
Kyo ware / 17th-18th century /
H 28.4cm / Tokyo National Museum

Porcelain Water Jar with Overglaze Enamel Design of Gayfeathers
Okuda Eisen / 19th-20th century /
MD 16.8cm / Tokyo National Museum

いろえ きりんきっか もんみずさし
色絵麒麟菊花文水指
奥田穎川 ／ 19〜20世紀 ／
口径 16.8cm ／ 東京国立博物館

Tiered Box with Handle , Underglaze Blue Design of Dragon and Wave
Aoki Mokubei / Important Cultural Property / 19th century /
H 23.0cm, D 23.0cm / Tokyo National Museum

そめつけりゅうとうもんさげじゅう
染付龍濤文提重
青木木米／重文／19世紀／
高23.0㎝　幅23.0㎝／東京国立博物館

**Covered Bowl with Overglaze Enamel Design
of Maple and Cherry Blossoms**
Nin'ami Dohachi / 1832-33 / MD 25.3cm /
Aichi Prefectural Ceramic Museum

<ruby>色<rt>いろ</rt>絵<rt>え</rt>雲<rt>うん</rt>錦<rt>きん</rt>手<rt>で</rt>蓋<rt>ふた</rt>物<rt>もの</rt></ruby>
色絵雲錦手蓋物
仁阿弥道八／1832〜33年
口径25.3cm／愛知県陶磁美術館

Stoneware Bowl with Three-color Glaze Design of Dragons
Eiraku Hozen / 19th century /
MD 17.3cm / Tokyo National Museum

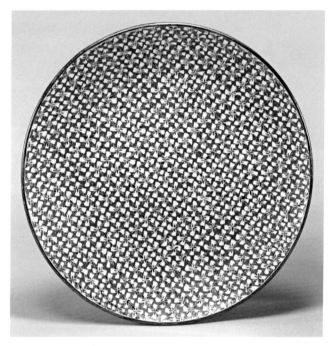

Large Dish with Chintz
Tomimoto Kenkichi / 20th century / MD 40.0cm /
Tokyo National Museum

いろえさらさもんおおざら
色絵更紗文大皿
富本憲吉／20世紀／
口径40.0cm／東京国立博物館

White Flat Jar of Grass and Flower Design, Ceramic, Glaze, Mold Making
Kawai Kanjiro / 1939 / H 33.0cm, D 30.0cm /
The National Museum of Modern Art, Kyoto

しろ じ くさばな え へん こ
白地草花絵扁壺
河井寛次郎／1939年／
高33.0cm 径30.0cm／京都国立近代美術館

Shigaraki Ware
(Shiga Prefecture)

Shigaraki was covered by a lake until approximately four million years ago and is blessed with rich clay propitious for pottery. When walking around Shigaraki, you may come across the ruins of the Shigaraki Palace constructed by Emperor Shomu (p. 124), as well as other places and names that recall ancient times, such as *Chokushi*, the imperial messenger. More than 1,250 years ago, Emperor Shomu ordered the firing of roof tiles and Sue ware, which initiated the history of Shigaraki ware. In the second half of the 16th century, masters of *Chanoyu* who favored the *Wabi-cha* style of tea ceremony started to use household utensils made of Shigaraki ware as tea utensils (see *Mitate*, p. 124). For instance, Uzukumaru, a masterpiece highly praised by masters of *Wabi-cha*, was originally made as a jar for storing seeds and later highly valued as a flower vase. Shigaraki ware is renowned for the beauty of its designs made by fire, including the "scarlet" of iron-rich soil, "*hai-kaburi*" grayish-brown of fired ash, the "vidro glaze" vitrified green by mixing ash with feldspar in the pottery clay, and the "dragonfly eyes" where the vidro glaze has hardened into a circle.

信楽焼（滋賀県）

　約400万年前は湖の底であった信楽は良質な陶土に恵まれている。信楽を巡ると、聖武天皇（p.124）の紫香楽（しがらき）宮跡をはじめ、勅使（ちょくし）など古（いにしえ）を感じる場所や地名が続く。1250年以上前に聖武天皇が瓦や須恵器を焼かせたのが信楽焼の始まり。16世紀後半には侘び茶を好む茶人の「見立て」（p.124）により、信楽焼の生活雑器を茶道具に使うようになる。たとえば、種入れだった壺を見立てに

Flower Vase Shaped Squat
Shigaraki ware / 16th century /
H 14.8cm / The Shigaraki Ceramic Cultural Park

より、花入れとした有名な古信楽「蹲（うずくまる）」など、茶陶としての名品が多い。陶土の鉄分が朱に発色した「火色（スカーレット）」、灰が灰褐色に発色した「灰かぶり」、灰が陶土内の白い粒（長石）と混ざり合って生じた緑色のガラス質の「ビードロ釉」、そのビードロ釉が丸く固まった「蜻蛉（とんぼ）の目」など、火が生む景色が美しい。

Water Jar with Straight Lip, Named "Shiba no Iori"
Shigaraki ware / Important Cultural Property /
16th-17th century /
H 14.7cm / Tokyo National Museum

<ruby>一<rt>ひと</rt></ruby><ruby>重<rt>え</rt></ruby><ruby>口<rt>ぐち</rt></ruby><ruby>水指<rt>みずさし</rt></ruby> <ruby>銘<rt>めい</rt></ruby> <ruby>柴庵<rt>しばのいおり</rt></ruby>
信楽／重文／16〜17世紀／
高14.7㎝／東京国立博物館

Kilns in Eastern Japan

本書で紹介する日本各地の窯場
(東海〜東日本)

①伊賀　②萬古　③美濃　④常滑
⑤瀬戸　⑥九谷　⑦越前　⑧益子
⑨笠間　⑩大堀相馬

Tamba-Tachikui Ware

(Hyogo Prefecture)

Tamba-Tachikui ware has been primarily produced in Tachikui, a village surrounded by mountains, in the southern part of Sasayama city in Hyogo Prefecture. Its history dates back a thousand years, when *yakishime* pots were fired inside pit kilns dug in the hillsides. The pottery was characterized by bright dark green natural glaze flowing over a brown earth surface. At the beginning of the 17th century, a semi-underground kiln was introduced from the Korean Peninsula, which enabled the mass production of glazed pottery. Then, at the end of the 17th century, a 50 meter-long "snake" kiln was constructed with holes at the top edge, called the "honeycomb," to let smoke out from inside the kiln. Even today, Tachikui village has the oldest existing snake kiln, established in 1895 and still in use several times a year. The Tamba Tachikui ware is often referred to as the "Seven Forms of Tamba" for the variety of ceramic techniques adopted for receptacles in daily use, among them sake bottles have been particoulary acclaimed.

丹波立杭焼 (兵庫県)

　兵庫県篠山市の南に位置する山あいの里、立杭を中心につくられてきたやきもの。歴史は1000年ほど前にさかのぼり、穴窯で焼締めの壺などがつくられた。赤褐色の土肌に鮮やかな濃緑色の自然釉が流れるのが特徴のやきものであった。17世紀の初めに、朝鮮半島から伝わった半地下登り窯が築かれるようになり、釉薬を使ったやきものが量産できるようになった。17世紀も終わりなると、全長が50mになる「蛇窯

Flower Vase with Round Decorations
Tanba ware / 17th century / H 25.9cm /
Tokyo National Museum

（じゃがま）」も築かれた。蛇窯の先端には「蜂の巣」と呼ばれる煙を出す穴がたくさん空けられている。今でも立杭の里には1895年に築かれた立杭最古の蛇窯があり、年に数回使われている。丹波立杭焼は「丹波の七化け」と称されるほど、多様な技法が使われた日用雑器が楽しめ、特に徳利が興味深い。

87

Iga Ware
(Mie Prefecture)

Iga, known overseas as the home of the Ninja, lies across a mountain from Shigaraki, and makes pottery using the high-quality ceramic clay of the old Lake Biwa. At the beginning of the 17th century, the master of *Chanoyu*, Furuta Oribe (p. 124), ordered the firing of water jugs and flower vases of Iga ware. The pottery produced in this period is called Koiga, which literally means ancient Iga. Koiga is characterized by a vidro glaze created by the firewood ash from trees such as the Japanese red pine which turns green while being fired in a kiln. Moreover, while it is being molded, Koiga is deliberately distorted and dented to create bold and dynamic shapes. With regards to Iga ware, it is often said that "Iga has ears, Shigaraki has none," which refers to Shigaraki ware's distinctive feature of the ear-shaped handles on the upper sides of pitchers and flower vases. Iga ware is excellent for heat and fire resistance, and is therefore suitable for making Yukihira pots and earthen pots, which are appreciated by many professional chefs. The finest features of Iga ware are "vidro glaze," "burnt," and "scarlet" which skilled artisans created in the pit kilns and climbing kilns.

伊賀焼 (三重県)

　　忍者の里として海外でも知られる伊賀は、信楽と山ひとつ隔てた地にあり、古琵琶湖層の良質な陶土を使ってやきものをつくっている。17世紀初頭には茶人の古田織部 (p.124) が好んで、伊賀焼で水指や花入れをつくらせた。この時代の伊賀焼は古伊賀と呼ばれ、窯で焼く際に、燃料となった赤松などの薪の灰が降りかかったところが緑色となったビードロ釉や、意識的に大きなゆがみやへこみをつくった大胆で豪快

耳付水指
<small>みみつきみずさし</small>
伊賀／17世紀／
高 19.5cm　口径 14.9cm ／東京国立博物館

Water Jar with Lugs
Iga ware / 17th century /
H 19.5cm, MD 14.9cm / Tokyo National Museum

な形が特徴。また「伊賀に耳あり、信楽に耳なし」といわれるように、水指や花入の上部に耳と呼ばれる装飾があることも、信楽とは異なる古伊賀の造形である。伊賀焼の土は、耐火性と耐熱性に優れているため、行平鍋や土鍋づくりに適しており、プロの料理人にもよく使われている。穴窯や登り窯の焼成が職人技の醍醐味で「ビードロ釉」「焦げ」「火色（スカーレット）」などの景色が楽しめる。

Banko Ware

(Mie Prefecture)

The Banko ware was initiated by Nunami Rouzan, who opened a kiln in 1736 and stamped his creations with the term "Banko-fueki" or "Banko" in the hope they would retain an eternal, never-changing life. Pottery from this period is called "old Banko ware." About thirty years after the death of Rouzan, Mori Yusetsu revived Banko ware. This is called "Yusetsu Banko" and became very popular for its cheerful design. At the end of the 19th century, the Shidei teapot was developed there. The iron-rich red clay of this region was used and fired without glaze, which changed the iron content of the pottery and turned it into a purplish-brown color. The longer a Shidei teapot is used, the more beautiful its luster becomes, which makes the pot ideal for *sencha* green tea. Moreover, the iron in the teapot is thought to absorb the tannin, a component of green tea, and reduce its bitter taste.

萬古焼 (三重県)

　萬古焼は1736年頃、沼波弄山 (ぬなみろうざん) が窯を開いたのが始まりで、弄山はやきものにいつまでも変わらない永遠の命を保つという願いを込めて「萬古不易 (ばんこふえき)」または「萬古」と印を押した。この時代のやきものは古萬古と呼ばれる。弄山が亡くなり、30年後森有節 (もりゆうせつ) が開窯し、萬古焼を再興する。煎茶の急須や斬新でキッチュな色あいのやきものが人気を集め、有節萬古と呼ばれた。19世紀の終わりには紫泥の急須が開発される。この地の鉄分の多い赤土を使い、釉薬をかけずに還元焼成すると、鉄分が変化して紫色を帯びた茶色に焼きあがる。紫泥急須は使えば使うほどに光沢がでてきて、煎茶にふさわしいものとなる。また緑茶の成分であるタンニンを急須の鉄分が吸収して、しぶみを和らげるともいわれている。

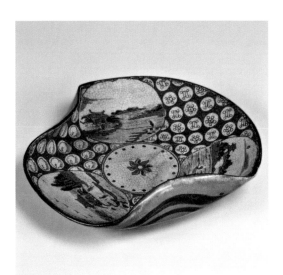

Dish with Overglaze Enamel Design of Landscape
Banko ware / 18th century /
H 6.1cm, D 23.3cm / Tokyo National Museum

Bowl with Overglaze Enamels
Mori Yusetsu I (or Ⅱ-Ⅲ) /
19th century /
H 8.5cm, MD 15.0cm /
Tokyo National Museum

いろえさんすいずまるもんさら
色絵山水図丸文皿
萬古／18世紀／
高6.1cm　径23.3cm／東京国立博物館
いろえばち
色絵鉢
初代森有節（あるいは2-3代）／19世紀／
高8.5cm　口径15.0cm／東京国立博物館

Chapter 5

Pottery
in
Eastern Japan

第五章

やきものめぐりの旅
東日本編

Mino Ware

(Gifu Prefecture)

Mino ware has a history of 1,300 years and the ruins of many kilns still remain in the Tono region where the Toki River flows through Gifu Prefecture. With the rise of *Chanoyu* in the 16th century, Shino, Kiseto, and Setoguro were born, which were much loved by masters of *Chanoyu*. In the 17th century, freely designed Oribe ware appeared due to the active interest of Oribe Furuta. Renowned for its milky-white color that can enchantingly melt one's heart, Shino ware further developed as Eshino ware and Nezumishino ware. While Eshino ware is decorated with underglaze iron patterns, Nezumishino is produced by applying iron coating to the entire surface, marking it with brush patterns, and then firing it with feldspar glaze (see *chosekiyu*, p. 124) to generate a mouse-grey color. With regard to the Kiseto accented with quaint russet, the patterns are gracefully designed using green of chalcanthite and brown of underglaze iron. Most Setoguro ware comprises ravishing black teacups, characterized by their right-angle shape. They are often referred to as "*hikidashi-guro* (drawer black)" from the act of removing from the kiln scalding pottery that has just been fired, so as to rapidly cool it down.

美濃焼 (岐阜県)

　やきものの生産量全国一を誇る美濃焼。1300年のやきものの歴史があるという美濃焼は、岐阜県の土岐川 (ときがわ) が流れる東濃地方にいくつもの窯跡が遺る。特に16世紀に入り、茶の湯が興隆していくとともに、茶人が愛してやまない志野、黄瀬戸、瀬戸黒などが生み出された。17世紀には茶人古田織部の好みで自由奔放な意匠の織部も生み出された。心を溶かす乳白色の志野には、鉄絵が描かれた「絵志

Shallow Bowl with Flowering Plants, Yellow Seto Type
Mino ware / 16th-17th century /
D 29.1cm / Tokyo National Museum

野」、鉄化粧を全面に施し、掻き落としで文様を表した後、長石釉 (p.124) をかけて
焼いた鼠色を呈する「鼠志野」などがある。趣のある朽葉色を呈した黄瀬戸は、胆
礬 (たんばん) の緑と鉄彩の茶で文様が描かれたものが床しい。漆黒の美の瀬戸黒
は茶碗が多く、ストンと直角な形が独特で、高温の窯から引き出して急冷させ漆黒に
なることから、「引き出し黒」と呼ばれることもある。

Setoguro Tea Bowl
Mino ware / 16th century / H 7.6cm, D 11.9-16.5cm /
Mino Ceramic Art Museum, Tane Electric Light Station Collection, Tajimi

<ruby>瀬<rt>せ</rt></ruby><ruby>戸<rt>と</rt></ruby><ruby>黒<rt>ぐろ</rt></ruby><ruby>茶<rt>ちゃ</rt></ruby><ruby>碗<rt>わん</rt></ruby>
瀬戸黒茶碗
美濃／16世紀／
高7.6cm 口径11.9〜16.5cm／多治見市
美濃焼ミュージアム 電燈所た襧コレクション

Bowl with a Wagtail, Nezumishino Type
Mino ware / Important Cultural Property /
16th-17th century / MD 28.5cm / Tokyo National Museum

鼠志野鶺鴒文鉢
美濃／重文／16〜17世紀／
口径28.5cm／東京国立博物館

Source: ColBas(https://colbase.nich.go.jp)　97

Bowl in the Shape of a Stylized Sandbank with a Handle, Oribe Type
Mino ware / 17th century /
H 17.7cm, D 22.0-24.5cm / Tokyo National Museum

Shoe-shaped Tea Bowl Named "Kakutaro", Kuro-oribe Type
Mino ware / 17th century /
MD 14.5cm / Tokyo National Museum

黒織部沓形茶碗 銘 鶴太郎
美濃／17世紀／
口径 14.5cm ／東京国立博物館

Tokoname Ware

(Aichi Prefecture)

Tokoname, located on the west side of the Chita Peninsula, is said to have had more than three thousand pit kilns in existence around 1100. Today Tokoname has become one of the centers of the Japanese ceramic industry for the production of sanitary ware. When you walk down the street which was used for firing clay pipes, looking at brick chimneys, you will come to the earthen slope lined with old clay pipes. As this area was covered by Lake Tokai approximately 6.5 million years ago, it yields fertile soil that contains fine particles rich in iron. This high-quality clay has enabled the application of the *yakishime* technique at low temperatures which is why large pots and bowls have been produced here since ancient times. Moreover, its favorable location for exporting led Tokoname to further prosper as a pottery production site. With the rise of *sencha* in the 19th century, teapots made with red clay mixed with iron oxide began to be produced and are still widely popular today. In the modern era, as clay pipes were required to construct a sewage system, Tokoname became a major production site for clay pipes.

常滑焼（愛知県）

　知多半島の西側にある常滑は1100年頃には、3000以上の穴窯が存在したという。現代は衛生陶器の生産が盛んな日本の窯業の中心地のひとつだ。レンガづくりの煙突を眺め、土管を焼くのに使った敷輪（けさわ）の上を歩くと、そこは古い土管が並べられた土管坂だ。このあたりは650万年前には東海湖の湖底であったため、鉄分が多く粒子の細かい陶土が産出される。この豊かな陶土は低温での焼き締めが可能だったので、古くから大きな壺や鉢が制作できたのである。また海上の輸送に適した地の利も、一層やきものを盛んにした。19世紀に煎茶が興隆すると、ベンガラを陶土に混ぜた朱泥を原料とした急須がつくられるようになり、今も人気だ。近代に入ると下水道を整備するために土管が必要になり、常滑は土管の一大生産地となった。

Water Jar with Lug, Natural Glaze
Tokoname ware / 13th century /
H 39.7cm, BD 41.0cm / Tokoname Tounomori Museum

Red Stoneware Pot
Yamada Jozan I /
19th-20th century /
H 6.3-6.5cm /
Tokoname Tounomori Museum

し ぜんゆうさん じ こ
自然釉三耳壺
常滑／13世紀／
高39.7cm　径41.0cm／とこなめ陶の森

常滑朱泥急須一双
初代山田常山／19〜20世紀／
高6.3〜6.5cm／とこなめ陶の森

Seto Ware

(Aichi Prefecture)

With a history of pottery that spans a thousand years, this area became a prodution center for pottery and then porcelain. The word "*Setomono*," which literally means a Seto item, became synonymous with pottery. In this area, there are many bridges that cross the Seto River, which are decorated with various kinds of ceramic tiles. The Azuma Bridge is decorated with Nezumishino, "mouse-colored" ceramic ware, while Kiseto, yellow-toned ceramic ware, is used for the Miyawaki Bridge. In addition, the Miyamae Bridge is decorated with cobalt-blue ware known as Sometsuki, and Oribe ware is the ceramic material used for the Minami Bridge. These colorful wares beautifully highlight the town as a pottery production site. The geological layer of this region is called the "Seto strata," which was deposited over ten million years ago. The clay in this area has exceptionally good thermal resistance and is easy to be casted. Moreover, Kibushi and Gairome clays—suitable for white ceramic wares—are found here. For this reason, Seto pottery was glazed with various colors and patterns since ancient times. Ceramic dolls and ornaments requiring fine craftsmanship were called "novelty," and were exported to Europe and the U.S. after WWⅡ, where they gained ample popularity.

瀬戸焼 (愛知県)

　1000年に及ぶやきものの歴史をもつこの地は、陶器に続いて磁器の産地ともなり、やがて「せともの」はやきものの代名詞となった。瀬戸川が流れるこの町には、鼠志野の東橋、黄瀬戸の宮脇橋、染付の宮前橋、織部の南橋など、陶板の橋が多く架かる。これらの橋からも、この地が多種多様なやきものの生産地であることが伺える。この町の地層は1000万年以上前から堆積してできた「瀬戸層群」。そこからは耐火性が高く成形しやすいうえに、白いやきものがつくれる陶土となる、木節 (きぶし) や蛙目 (がいろめ) 粘土が採取できた。そのため古くから釉薬をかけてさまざまな色や文様を施すことが可能だったのだ。細かな技巧が必要な陶磁器製の人形や装飾品は「ノベルティ」と呼ばれ、第二次世界大戦後、欧米に輸出され人気を博した。

Flower Vase with Underglaze Blue Design of Flowers
Kawamoto Masukichi / 19th-20th century /
H 30.5cm each / Aichi Prefectural Ceramic Museum

**Ornament,
"Lady Catching a Fish"**
Seto ware / 1948 / H 34.0cm /
Aichi Prefectural
Ceramic Museum

染付草花文花瓶 一対
川本枡吉／19〜20世紀／
左右ともに高30.5㎝／愛知県陶磁美術館

ノベルティ「魚取りをする女性」
瀬戸／1948年
高34.0㎝／愛知県陶磁美術館

Kutani Ware

(Ishikawa Prefecture)

During only half a century, from the mid 17th century to the early 18th century, beautiful pottery known as Ko-Kutani was created, which still fascinates people today. The decorated porcelain is almost like a painting, using bold and free designs colored by glossy pigments. The surface of this decorated pottery is glazed either by the five-colored style known as Gosai-de, using red, blue (or green), yellow, purple, and Prussian blue, or another style known as Ao-de, using two or three colors from the five colors of Gosai-de, except red. The production of Kutani ware was revived in the 19th century, inviting distinguished pottery artist Aoki Mokubei to Kyoto to produce Aka-e Gosu porcelain depicting Chinese-style birds and flowers at the Kasugayama kiln. Also, the main Kutani kiln invited Eiraku Wazen of the Eiraku family in Kyoto, a member of the Senke Jisshoku (the ten distinguished families of tea ware craftsmen), to produce pottery with gold glazing. Since the opening of Japan after the isolation policy, Kutani ware became highly popular abroad as Japan Kutani. In particular, the gold technique known as "*saishiki-kinrande*" by Kutani Shoza made Kutani ware famous throughout the world.

九谷焼（石川県）

17世紀半ばから18世紀の初頭まで、わずかな半世紀のあいだに、今なお人々を魅了してやまない古九谷と呼ばれる美しいやきものがつくられた。その色絵磁器はまるで絵画のようで、大胆で自由な意匠が艶やかな色彩で描かれる。赤、青（緑）、黄、紫、紺青が使われた五彩手と、青手（五彩手から赤を除いた色彩のうち、2色か3色のみを使った）の上絵つけのやきものだ。19世紀に入り、九谷焼は再興される。京都の

Large Dish with Overglaze Enamel Design of Peony and Butterfly
Old Kutani Style / 17century / D 35.0cm / Tokyo National Museum

名工としても名高い青木木米を招き、中国風の花鳥などを写した赤絵呉須を春日山窯でつくるようになる。また九谷本窯では現在千家十職（せんけじっしょく）の永楽家の12代永楽和全を招き、金彩のやきものをつくり始めた。日本が開国されると九谷焼は海外でジャパンクタニとして人気を博すようになり、特に九谷庄三（くたにしょうざ）の彩色金襴手は九谷焼の名を世界に知らしめた。

Shallow Bowl with Overglaze Enamel Design of Cranes
Yoshida-ya kiln / 19th century /
D 39.0cm / Ishikawa Prefectural Museum of Art

Bowl with Overglaze Red Enamel Design of Flowers and Birds
Miyamoto-ya kiln / 19th century /
MD 21.4cm / Ishikawa Prefectural Museum of Art

<ruby>赤<rt>あか</rt>絵<rt>え</rt>花<rt>か</rt>鳥<rt>ちょう</rt>文<rt>もん</rt>鉢<rt>ばち</rt></ruby>
宮本屋窯／19世紀／
口径21.4cm／石川県立美術館

**Large Incense Burner with Overglaze Enamel and
Gold Design of Flowers and Birds**
Kutani Shoza / 1878 /
H 32.6cm, MD 22.3cm / Ishikawa Prefectural Museum of Art

いろえ きんさい か ちょうもんおおごう ろ
色絵金彩花鳥文大香炉
九谷庄三 ／ 1878 年 ／
高 32.6cm　口径 22.3cm ／ 石川県立美術館

**Gourd-shaped Sake Bottle with Overglaze Red Enamel and
Gold Design of Dragon**
Asai Ichimo / 20th century / H 18.0cm /
Ishikawa Prefectural Museum of Art

あか え きんさいりゅうもんひさごがたとっくり
赤絵金彩龍文瓢形徳利
浅井一毫／20世紀／
高18.0㎝／石川県立美術館

Echizen Ware
(Fukui Prefecture)

Echizen, the center of Echizen ware, is a snowy region where the climate is so extreme that even the soil freezes through the winter season. During the second half of the 12th century, Echizen became famous for its pottery, and ruins of its former ceramic sites still remain around the Ozowara area. The clay in this area is highly refractory due to the vitreous nature of the soil. Its glassy materials melt with high temperatures, filling the gaps between particles of the clay and eventually enabling the production of large size, robust pottery with a lustrous surface. The coiling technique of Echizen, known as "*Echizen nejitate giho*," is a special skill that has been passed down since the Middle Ages. To make large-sized pots and jars, the artisan wraps thick clay strands around the edge of the base and builds up several levels of the clay string while walking. Then, moving in the opposite direction, the piled clay is stretched upwards with a wooden iron to smooth the surface. This process is repeated to pile the clay, with the mouth of the piece formed last. The traditional art of Echizen ware has a sturdy shape and an earthy texture made by *yakishime*, which is truly fascinating.

越前焼（福井県）

　越前焼の中心である越前町は冬になると雪が多く、土も凍るほどの厳しい風土である。12世紀後半からやきものの産地となり、その頃の遺跡は越前町小曽原周辺に分布する。この近辺の陶土は耐火度が高くガラス質を多く含むために、高温で焼くと土のガラス質が溶けて粒子の隙間を埋め、光沢があり硬く焼締まった大きなやきものづくりが可能であった。「越前捻じたて技法」は中世から受け継がれている技である。

Jar
Echizen ware / 15th century / H 47.2cm /
Aichi Prefectural Ceramic Museum

人が大きな壺や甕をつくるために底部の縁を回り歩いて太い粘土の紐を積んでいき、つぎに逆方向に回りながら、木のこてで粘土を下から上へ引き伸ばし、粘土のつなぎ目を消していく。こういった作業を繰り返し、粘土を高く積み上げ、最後には器の口の部分を仕上げる。越前焼の伝統技の器は、どっしりとした焼締めの土肌が魅力だ。

Mashiko Ware

(Tochigi Prefecture)

It was nearly the end of the 18th century when pottery began to be produced in Mashiko, and it was not until the middle of the 20th century that the contemporary style of the Mashiko ware was established. It is no exaggeration to state that Hamada Shoji single-handedly determined the thick, heavy, and warm image of Mashiko ware. He was one of Japan's leading modern potters and he is also well-known abroad, along with Yanagi Soyetsu, who promoted the *Mingei* movement. In 1920, Hamada traveled to England with potter Bernard Leach, and there began his career as a pottery artist. Hamada himself later said, "I found my way in Kyoto, started my career in England, studied in Okinawa, and grew up in Mashiko." After returning to Japan, he moved to Mashiko in 1924 and continued to create works using Mashiko clay and glazing. Approximately 150 years ago, there was a large lake in Mashiko and the soil at the bottom of that lake provides the clay for Mashiko ware. For the glazing, locally available materials, such as melted Ashinuma stone, are also used.

益子焼（栃木県）

　益子の地でやきものがつくられるようになったのは1852年頃、また現代の益子焼のイメージが出来上がったのは、20世紀も半ば近くになってからだ。益子焼の厚手でどっしりとした温かみのあるイメージは、濱田庄司によってつくられたといっても過言ではない。濱田は日本の近現代を代表する陶芸家のひとりであるが、民藝運動を推し進めた柳宗悦とともに、海外でも名の知られた作家である。濱田は1920年に陶芸家

Flower Vase with Overglazed Reddish-brown Glaze
Hamada Shoji / Mashiko Museum of Ceramic Art

バーナード・リーチとともにイギリスへ渡り、作家としての活動を始めた。濱田自身が
「京都で道をみつけ、英国で始まり、沖縄で学び、益子で育った」と、後に語ってい
るように、帰国後の1924年に益子に居を移し、益子の土を活かした作品をつくり続
けた。釉薬にも地元の芦沼石（あしぬまいし）を溶かしたものなどが使われている。

Kasama Ware

(Ibaraki Prefecture)

Kasama ware was initiated in the late 18th century and is the oldest form of pottery in the Kanto region. The clay of Kasama ware is mined from the Yamizo Mountains. It is viscous, with a very fine-grained texture and when fired it becomes hard and solid, making it suitable to produce pottery for everyday use. As shown in the photograph, traditional Kasama ware is characterized by a blue and amber-colored glaze over a white rice bran glaze. When Hamada Shoji moved to Mashiko in 1930 and the *Mingei* Movement became more active, many artists began to gather in Mashiko. Kasama, on the other hand, began to attract artists who did not fit into the existing framework of Japanese folk art. As a result, it produced a number of historically significant potters, including Itaya Hazan (p. 125) in the second half of the 19th century and Matsui Kosei (p. 125) in the second half of the 20th century, who elevated local pottery to an art form. The diversity of modern Kasama ware is the product of local people's open-mindedness, their appreciation of the individuality of the artists who gathered there, allowing them to create in their own free style.

笠間焼（茨城県）

　笠間焼は18世紀後半に開窯され、関東では最古の歴史を誇る。笠間焼の陶土は八溝山地（やみぞさんち）から採っており、その土はきめ細やかで粘り強く、焼成すると、固く焼き締まり、堅牢になるため、日用品としてのやきものに適している。写真のように糠白釉に青釉と飴釉を流し掛けるのが伝統的な笠間焼の特徴である。1930年に濱田庄司が益子に移り、民藝運動が活発になると、益子に多くの作家が集まるようにな

Jar with Bran White Glaze and Trailed Copper Glaze
Kasama ware / Late 19th century-Early 20th century /
Ibaraki Ceramic Art Museum

った。一方、笠間には民芸の枠にはまらない作家が集まるようになる。19世紀後半には板谷波山（p.125）、20世紀後半には松井康成（p.125）など歴史に名を遺す作家を輩出し、この地のやきものを芸術の域にまで高めた。現在の多種多様な笠間焼は、この地に集まる作家の個性を大切にし、自由な作風でつくらせる人々の懐の深さから引き起こされたものであり、それこそが現代の笠間焼の特徴といえるだろう。

Obori-Soma Ware

(Fukushima Prefecture)

The birthplace of Obori-Soma ware is located near an area called Obori in the town of Namie, Fukushima Prefecture. Its production began at the end of the 17th century and by the end of the 18th century became one of the largest sites for pottery production in the Tohoku region. However, the number of pottery producers in the area has been decreasing and, after the Great East Japan Earthquake in 2011, was designated as an evacuation zone, forcing the twenty-five remaining potters to close down. Eleven pottery studios are currently aiming to revive their operations in Fukushima, Nihonmatsu, Koriyama, Minami-Soma, Aizu, Aichi, and Oita. Traditional Obori-Soma ware, with a history of 300 years, is made from a locally available Toyamaishi stone, with a bluish celadon glaze and crackles known as "*ao-hibi*," or blue crackles, covering its entire surface. Another important characteristic of Obori-Soma ware is the depiction of horses known as "*hashiri-koma* (running horse)" or "*hidari uma* (left horse)", a unique design exclusively seen in this area. The artisans of Obori-Soma ware are recognized as full-fledged potters when they perfected the art of capturing the dynamic movement of the horses as if galloping on the ceramic surface.

大堀相馬焼 (福島県)

　大堀相馬焼の故郷は福島県浪江町の大堀あたりだ。17世紀の終わりに始まり、18世紀の終わりごろには東北地方で最も大きなやきものの産地となった。しかしながら近現代になり生産者が減り続け、2011年の東日本大震災で被災し、帰宅困難区域に指定されてしまった。そのため当時残っていた25件の窯元も離散せざるをえなくなり、現在は11軒の窯元が福島、二本松、郡山、南相馬、会津、愛知、大分など県

Gourd-shaped Bottle with Design of Horse
Soma ware / 18th-19th century /
H 30.6cm, MD 4.4cm / Aichi Prefectural Ceramic Museum

内外で再興をめざしている。300年の歴史をもつ伝統的な大堀相馬焼は、この地の砥山石からつくられた透明な青みのある青磁釉がかけられた陶器であり、「青ひび」と呼ばれる貫入が全体を覆っている。またこの地独特の「走り駒」「左馬」と呼ばれる馬の絵が描かれていることも大きな特徴だ。この馬に躍動感が宿り、今にも走り出しそうに描けるようになると大堀相馬焼の一人前の職人となる。

Appendix

Glossary

付録

用語集

Glossary | 用語集

Yuyaku

釉薬 ゆうやく

Yuyaku, or ceramic glaze, is a glassy layer of film that covers the surface of earthenware. Originally, ash from the firewood in the kiln fused with the minerals in the ceramic pieces to form a vitreous layer, or a natural glaze. This spurred an endless array of manual glazes, incorporating plant ash and natural minerals.

やきものの表面を覆うガラス質の膜のこと。焼成の過程で燃料となる薪の灰が土の成分と融合して生まれたガラス質の層（自然釉）から学び、植物の灰や鉱物を用いてさまざまな釉薬を開発し、人工的に用いるようになった。

Anagama

穴窯 あながま

An *anagama*, or pit kiln, is a single chamber kiln dug in the ground or on a slope. Introduced from the Korean Peninsula in the 5th century, its enclosed configuration ensured that the temperature, once risen, would last the entire firing process.

焼成温度が上がって、十分に焼き締まるように、地中に穴を掘ってつくった窯、または斜面に縦に溝を掘って天井をかぶせた窯のこと。5世紀に朝鮮半島から伝わった。

Noborigama

登り窯 のぼりがま

A *noborigama*, or climbing kiln, denotes a chain of firing chambers dug on sloping ground. Heat from the firebox at the bottom streams through each successive chamber to the top. This technology is believed to have traveled from the Korean Peninsula around the 17th century, making it possible to fire porcelain.

傾斜地を利用して穴を掘ってつくられた複数の小部屋をもつ細長い窯。下のほうの焚き口で薪を燃やし、上へ伝わる熱を利用する仕組み。17世紀頃に朝鮮半島から伝わったといわれ、磁器の焼成も可能にした。

Sen no Rikyu (1522-91)

Sen no Rikyu was born into a wealthy family in Sakai, Osaka. A master of *Chanoyu* during the Azuchi-Momoyama period, his perfection of the *Wabi-cha* aesthetics has had a profound and lasting effect on tea ceremony and its *Kogei* (life tools of practical and aesthetic value, such as ceramics and lacquer ware).

Chapter 2

Tomimoto Kenkichi (1886-1963)

Born in Nara, Tomimoto Kenkichi graduated in architecture from the Tokyo Fine Arts School. Tomimoto was inspired by William Morris during his subsequent studies in London. He returned to Japan and forged an enduring ceramic friendship with Bernard Leach. Tomimoto was distinguished as an Intangible Cultural Property for his colored porcelain.

Chapter 3

Yohen

Scorched surface coloring is a random change that occurs to a piece during firing. It can be caused by conditions in the kiln such as amount of heat, type of firewood and type of glaze.

千利休
せんのりきゅう
（1522〜91）

大坂・堺生まれの茶人。侘び茶の完成者であり、彼の美意識はその後の茶の湯と工芸（陶芸、漆芸など、実用性と美的価値をそなえた生活用品）に大きな影響を与えた。

第二章

富本憲吉
とみもとけんきち
（1886〜1963）

奈良県に生まれ。東京美術学校（現・東京藝術大学）建築科卒業後、ロンドンに留学、ウィリアム・モリスの影響を受ける。帰国後バーナード・リーチとの交流を通して、ともに陶芸の道に進んだ。色絵磁器の重要無形文化財保持者。

第三章

窯変 ようへん

火の加減や薪の種類、釉薬の種類など、さまざまな条件によって、窯の中で偶然生じる色相変化のこと。

Kushigaki

Kushigaki is a technique of decorating multiple parallel lines or wavy patterns using a comb-shaped tool with many separate tips. The lines are engraved while the base material is soft, but the pattern varies depending on the depth and shape of the comb pattern. The comb pattern changes the condition of the glaze and creates a glaze pool, which results in tasteful decoration.

Bernard Leach (1887-1979)

Bernard Leach was a studio potter, an Englishman born in Hong Kong, who spent his early years in Japan. He returned to Japan at the age of twenty-two, whereupon he began to study Japanese ceramics, being so smitten by the art. Leach was involved in the early days of the *Mingei* Folk Art Movement along with his close acquaintances, Yanagi Soyetsu and Tomimoto Kenkichi. Leach saw his role as a messenger of East and West ceramic traditions and he gave an important contribution to the world's ceramic industry.

Himotsukuri

Coiling is a basic molding technique. Coils of clay are stacked on the rim of

櫛描き くしがき

素地に先端が多数に分かれている櫛形の道具を使って複数の平行線や波形の文様などを装飾する技法。素地が柔らかいうちに線刻を彫るが、櫛目の深さや形状によっては文様が異なる。櫛描きによって釉薬の調子が変化し釉だまりなどができ、趣きのある装飾となる。

バーナード・リーチ
(1887～1979)

香港生まれ。幼少の頃に日本で過ごしたイギリス人。22歳で再来日し、日本の陶芸に魅了される。柳宗悦、富本憲吉に出会い、民藝運動にかかわった。東洋と西洋の間の使者と自らを位置づけ、世界の陶芸界に貢献した。

紐つくり

成形の基本的な技。器の土台（底部）外周に、紐状の粘土を巻き上げるように積み上げて成形し、つなぎ目を手でならして表裏を滑らかに整える技法。

a base and smoothed out by hand to create the walls of a vessel.

Chapter 4

Hon'ami Koetsu (1558-1637)

Hon'ami Koetsu was a definitive Kyoto artist. Though his family trade was sword polishing and appraising, he left behind a vast number of calligraphic and ceramic masterpieces.

Ogata Kenzan (1663-1743)

Ogata Kenzan was a potter and painter, the son of a wealthy Kyoto kimono merchant. He studied ceramics under Nonomura Ninsei, drawn by the master's colorful porcelain. Kenzan often collaborated with his older brother, Ogata Korin, a highly acclaimed painter, on the ornamentation of his pottery. He moved to Edo, nowadays Tokyo, in his latter years, where he established his own kiln.

Nin'ami Dohachi (1783-1855)

Nin'ami was a second-generation Kyoto potter of the Takahashi Dohachi family. He came to the fore after honing his skills under the tutelage of Okuda Eisen. A master of the Rinpa style, his exquisite copies of Ninsei and Kenzan tea ceremony masterpieces are legend.

第四章

本阿弥光悦
ほんあみこうえつ
（1558～1637）

京都を代表する美術家。刀剣の鑑定・研磨を家職とする一方で、書や陶芸に秀で数々の傑作を遺した。

尾形乾山
おがたけんざん
（1663～1743）

京都の呉服屋に生まれる。野々村仁清の色絵磁器に魅せられ、陶技を学ぶ。兄の尾形光琳が絵付し、乾山が作陶する合作を多く遺す。晩年は江戸に出て窯を築いた。

仁阿弥道八
にんなみどうはち
（1783～1855）

京都生まれ。やきものを生業とする高橋道八家の2代目。奥田穎川に師事し、陶技を磨く。琳派風の意匠を得意とし、仁清や乾山などの写しも多く作陶している。

Emperor Shomu (701-756)

Emperor Shomu, the 45th emperor, was an ardent Buddhist who built the Todaiji Temple and cast the Great Buddha. Buddhist art of this period is called Tenpyo culture and boasts splendid skill. The relics of Emperor Shomu still exist as treasures in the Shosoin Repository, located on the grounds of the Todaiji Temple.

Mitate

To represent a form not in the way it was intended, but for something else.

Furuta Oribe (1543-1615)

Furuta Oribe, a tea master from Mino. Though a distinguished disciple of Sen no Rikyu, he formed his own innovative Oribe-style tea ceremony. He popularized his "Oribe taste" in design, for which Oribe-yaki is especially famous.

Chapter 5

Chosekiyu

The glaze is primarily made using feldspar—a mineral containing silicic acid that turns into a white glaze when a small amount of ash is added. As feldspar has a high melting

---

聖武天皇
しょうむてんのう
(701〜756)

第45代天皇。仏教に深く帰依し、東大寺を建立、大仏を鋳造した。この時期の仏教芸術は天平文化と呼ばれ、高い技の華麗な工芸品を誇る。聖武天皇の遺品は正倉院宝物として現存する。

見立て

対象となるものを、別のものになぞらえて表現すること。

古田織部
ふるたおりべ
(1543〜1615)

美濃生まれの武将、茶人。千利休の高弟であったが、独自の豪放な織部流の茶道を成す。「織部好み」の意匠を流行させ、なかでも特徴の織部焼は有名。

第五章

長石釉 ちょうせきゆう

主な材料である長石は珪酸を含んだ鉱物で、灰を少し加えると白釉となる。長石は溶解温度が高く、ひびや気泡ができやすいため、その特徴も志野によくでるのである。

temperature and can easily develop crackles and air bubbles, such characteristics are often seen in Shino.

Itaya Hazan (1872-1963)

Itaya Hazan, a widely acclaimed pioneer of modern Japanese ceramics, was born in Ibaraki Prefecture and graduated in sculpture from the Tokyo Fine Arts School. He embraced the world of ceramics while teaching it at a school in Ishikawa Prefecture. The shallow relief and delicate coloring of his works intone his elegant style.

Matsui Kosei (1927-2003)

A native of Nagano Prefecture, Matsui Kosei became head chief priest of an old temple in Kasama, Ibaraki, where he later installed a kiln. There, he mastered the *neriage* technique of producing an array of patterns by combining two or more types of clay of differing properties. His mastery earned him recognition as an Intangible Cultural Property for his *neriage* technique.

板谷波山
いたやはざん
(1872～1963)

茨城県生まれ。東京美術学校彫刻科を卒業後、石川県の学校で陶磁を教え、作陶の道に進む。薄彫（うすぼり）で繊細な彩色の格調高い作風が特徴。

松井康成
まついこうせい
(1927～2003)

長野県生まれ。笠間市で古刹の住職となったのち、境内に窯を設けると、性質の異なる2種類以上の土を用いて、さまざまな模様を表現する練上技法を極めた。練上（ねりあげ）の重要無形文化財保持者。

澤田美恵子　さわだ・みえこ

京都工芸繊維大学教授。博士（言語文化学）。
工芸評論家（https://www.lovekogei.com）。
京都市生まれ。大阪外国語大学大学院修了後、
グルノーブル大学（フランス）講師、神戸大学助教授、
京都工芸繊維大学准教授を経て現職。
著書に『工芸バイリンガルガイド』（小学館）、
『やきもの そして 生きること』（理論社）、
共著に『京の工芸ものがたり』（理論社）、
『工芸の四季』（京都新聞出版センター）など多数。

編集協力
齊藤尚美（くるみ企画室）

装丁・本文デザイン
金田一亜弥　髙畠なつみ（金田一デザイン）

用語集英訳
Mae Nagai

和文校正
兼古和昌

協力
日本児童教育振興財団FAJE

Bilingual Guide to Japan
JAPANESE POTTERY

やきものバイリンガルガイド

2020 年 12 月 5 日　初版　第 1 刷発行
2024 年 5 月 27 日　　　　第 2 刷発行

著　者　澤田美恵子
発行者　斎藤　満
発行所　株式会社小学館
　　　　〒 101 - 8001
　　　　東京都千代田区一ツ橋 2 - 3 - 1
　　　　編集 03 - 3230 - 5563　販売 03 - 5281 - 3555

印刷所　大日本印刷株式会社
製本所　株式会社若林製本工場
ＤＴＰ　株式会社昭和ブライト

編　集　矢野文子（小学館）

©2020 Mieko Sawada, Naomi Saito
Printed in Japan
ISBN 978-4-09-388795-3